Child Protection and Safeguarding Technologies

This book explores, through a children's rights-based perspective, the emergence of a safeguarding dystopia in child online protection that has emerged from a tension between an over-reliance in technical solutions and a lack of understanding around code and algorithm capabilities. The text argues that a safeguarding dystopia results in docile children, rather than safe ones, and that we should stop seeing technology as the sole solution to online safeguarding.

The reader will, through reading this book, gain a deeper understanding of the current policy arena in online safeguarding, what causes children to become upset online, and the doomed nature of safeguarding solutions. The book also features a detailed analysis of issues surrounding content filtering, access monitoring, surveillance, image recognition, and tracking.

This book is aimed at legal practitioners, law students, and those interested in child safeguarding and technology.

Andy Phippen is a Professor of Social Responsibility in Information Technology at the University of Plymouth. He has specialised in the use of ICTs in social contexts for almost 20 years, carrying out a large amount of grassroots research on issues such as privacy and data protection, and internet safety and contemporary social concerns like sexting, peer abuse, and the impact of digital technology on wellbeing. He has presented written and oral evidence to parliamentary inquiries related to the use of ICTs in society, is widely published in the area, and is a frequent media commentator on these issues.

Maggie Brennan is a research psychologist, based at the School of Applied Psychology, University College Cork.

Child Protection and Safeguarding Technologies

Appropriate or Excessive 'Solutions' to Social Problems?

Andy Phippen and Maggie Brennan

Routledge
Taylor & Francis Group

LONDON AND NEW YORK

First published 2020
by Routledge
2 Park Square, Milton Park, Abingdon, Oxon OX14 4RN

and by Routledge
605 Third Avenue, New York, NY 10017

First issued in paperback 2021

Routledge is an imprint of the Taylor & Francis Group, an informa business

Publisher's Note
The publisher has gone to great lengths to ensure the quality of this reprint but points out that some imperfections in the original copies may be apparent.

British Library Cataloguing-in-Publication Data
A catalogue record for this book is available from the British Library

Library of Congress Cataloging-in-Publication Data
A catalog record has been requested for this book

Typeset in Galliard
by Deanta Global Publishing Services, Chennai, India

ISBN 13: 978-1-03-224048-0 (pbk)
ISBN 13: 978-1-138-55540-2 (hbk)

DOI: 10.4324/9781315149493

Contents

Illustrations

Figures

Tables

1   Doing more to safeguard children online

> Governments of the Industrial World, you weary giants of flesh and steel, I come from Cyberspace, the new home of Mind. On behalf of the future, I ask you of the past to leave us alone. You are not welcome among us. You have no sovereignty where we gather.

This quotation is taken from John Perry Barlow's "Declaration of Independence for Cyberspace"[1], a much-cited *manifesto* that claimed Governments would always fail to control the online world. The declaration was written on the day the US Telecommunications Act 1996 came into force[2]. While the US government claimed this act would introduce great competition to the telecommunications infrastructure market, those who opposed it claimed it would consolidate power into the hands of a few major corporations (which turned out to be true). *Internet Libertarians*, who wished for a free and neutral digital world, felt these early attempts to control online communications and place it in a competitive space were doomed to fail, with the declaration continuing:

> Cyberspace does not lie within your borders. Do not think that you can build it, as though it were a public construction project. You cannot. It is an act of nature and it grows itself through our collective actions.

Yet, over 20 years after this declaration, we still see many attempts to *regulate* the online world – applying geographically distinct legislation to a global phenomenon that evolved and emerged through convergence and mutual interest, rather than commercial interests and market forces. Commerce and governments only discovered the Internet once it was established, and therefore had little chance to exploit it or regulate it as it grew. This declaration does bring attention to an interesting tension between online technology and the need for governments to govern and pass legislation that protects citizens from potential harms and regulates their antisocial behaviour. We would not take exception to this. The Declaration of Independence for Cyberspace is not so much a claim that *anything* that happens online cannot be regulated, more that trying to legislate to change the infrastructure and technology of the online environment will neither achieve its aims or be effective legislature.

One of the areas where this is very apparent is child protection and safeguarding, where, understandably, governments wish to mitigate risk for young people going online, and to ensure they are *safe*. We should state, from the outset of this text, that we are absolutely supportive of the need for child protection and safeguarding legislation that is effective at providing effective safeguards for children and young people in all aspects of their lives, ensuring they can grow up and live their lives while minimising the risk of harm. However, within this text we will explore that if governments are attempting to "control" online behaviour by tackling it at the wrong level – we use the UK as a case study in the tension between policy and technology – just because there is problematic behaviour online, it does not necessarily follow that technology will be able to address this or even that the technology exists to implement what is demanding in policy documents and legislation.

We are reminded of Marcus Ranum's much-quoted Law[3]:

> You can't solve social problems with software.

This is not a policy book, this has been covered in detailed elsewhere[4]. It is instead an exploration of what happens when policy and technology collide, arguably for a common purpose, and what happens when policy makers fail to understand the technologies they wish to *control*. If you will, it is more a book that critically explores the nature of algorithms in the online child safeguarding space, against a backdrop of increasing regulatory pressure.

It presents a rationale behind why policy tends to address online concerns with demands on the technologies themselves, and argues that an overreliance is actually detrimental to child development and children's rights. It also considers whether safeguarding is actually at the heart of technology *solutions* or whether we are sleepwalking into an environment that is more concerned with control and achieving docility rather than safety.

If we consider the raw material of the online world, software code, and its more aggregate form, algorithms, we can better understand why online behaviour is such a challenge for governments to regulate and therefore why they will, instead, try to pass the buck to those who implement technology, arguably because this is easier than challenging the more complex aspects of society that are merely reflected online, rather than facilitated by it.

Since the inception of online technology and its development into a powerful and global communications network, governments have tried to control it. Yet they rarely succeed. While there have been some pioneering legal texts that explain the complexities of the regulation of the online world, it would seem that policy makers fail to acknowledge this discourse. Lawrence Lessig, in his seminal work[5], laid out a very clear and provocative argument around efforts to regulate the online world and how controlling behaviour online is not possible, due to the nature of the environment in which this behaviour took place.

> The claim for cyberspace was not just that government would not regulate cyberspace—it was that government could not regulate cyberspace.

Cyberspace was, by nature, unavoidably free. Governments could threaten, but behavior could not be controlled; laws could be passed, but they would have no real effect.

Lessig argued that in order for a regulatory environment to be a success, there were four key *modalities*, one being *laws* but there were also *social norms, market*, and *architecture*. All of these had a significant role to play in managing and regulating society for the benefit of all. Within the physical world, these modalities work, because they are clear and adhere to natural law (physics, biology, acceptable moralities), and legislation works, because it can be applied to a physical space (i.e. a country) without ambiguity. Within the online world, the only *architecture* that exists is *code*, the raw material of digital technology[6], and the hardware upon which the code communicates. This code designed, written, and shaped by those with the skills, knowledge, and talent to be able to turn the requirements of users into functional algorithms and assemble them into software platforms. Lessig's primary idea is that code becomes, in essence, the law of the online world, because it is the only way *rules* can be implemented. However, there are boundaries to what code can achieve, constrained by logic and the implementation of biases of those who implement it. Code cannot implement ambiguity, imprecision, or interpretation. It, or more accurately, coders, can only implement things that can be defined in a logical manner, and this presents significant challenges when tackling social issues, where system boundaries can be infinity and behaviour is unpredictable.

Governments and policy makers are aware that they have little chance to implement legislation that can effectively control the online world – they cannot impose national rules on something that has no national boundaries. Therefore, it is little surprise that they turn instead to those who can implement rules on the networks and decide instead that their legislation will ensure the technology providers themselves will sort out the social problems that arise in online spaces. And while one might hope that mutual interest might mean that a harmonious goal could achieve something as mutually agreeable as child safeguarding, increasingly the tension between governments and industry result in a conflict between these two stakeholders – "stop this from happening, or we will legislate".

This can be clearly seen in the current age verification debate in the UK. Legislation has been established[7] that mandates providers whose services provide commercial access to pornography must implement age verification technology such as to ensure no UK citizen under the age of 18 can access this content. We will explore this particular "solution" in far more detail in Chapter 3, but highlight it here as a demonstration of an expectation that industry must find a way, regardless of whether the architecture, social norms, or market forces exist to make it possible.

To take this seemingly simple example, let us consider how we might prevent children from accessing pornography. From a logical perspective, there are two main requirements in order to achieve this:

1. We know the age of the end user
2. We know that a piece of content is pornographic

If we can achieve this, we can prevent children from accessing such content. However, if we take each point in turn:

1. Unless we have some means for all citizens to be able to demonstrate their age in a digital form how do we know their age?
2. Can we define, in logic, what makes a piece of content pornographic, if we cannot even define it in law? While attempts to define in law do exist, and will be discussed later, these are of themselves ambiguous, and the subject of much case law. If this is the case, how might we expect an algorithm to determine whether one of a potentially massive volume of online content, contains pornographic material?

When we make calls for what sounds simple from a legislative perspective, we need to appreciate the complexities of providing this in code where logic needs to be precise and unambiguous, and leave no room for subjectivity. Reidenberg's work on the *Lex Informatica*[8] very clearly pointed out the need for this understanding. He argued that digital technology imposes its own rules on how data is communicated, and what is possible in this management:

> The pursuit of technological rules that embody flexibility for information flows maximizes public policy options; at the same time, the ability to embed an immutable rule in system architecture allows for the preservation of public-order values. These tools can lessen a number of problems that traditional legal solutions face in regulating the Information Society. Yet a shift in public policy planning must occur in order for Lex Informatica to develop as an effective source of information policy rules. The new institutions and mechanisms will not be those of traditional government regulation. Policymakers must begin to look to Lex Informatica to effectively formulate information policy rules.

Put simply, code is good at some things, and poor at others, and the public policy space needs to understand where these strengths and weaknesses lie in order to make effective legislation to tackle social issues. And they also need to understand that code cannot solve *everything*.

This book centres on technologies, mainly algorithms but also some application of hardware in tandem with code, that are used in child protection and safeguarding. It draws upon experiences from authors who have written code, taught software development and computer ethics (and social responsibility), and also engaged extensively at a grassroots level in the online child safeguarding arena – primarily working with children and young people to better understand how they use technology, which risks they are exposed to, and their wishes for their safeguarding. This is carried out in a number of observational and immersive approaches: working in classrooms, conducting workshops, and even doing presentations in school assemblies to gain a deep appreciation of the sorts of discourse around what they, the young people, enjoy online, how they are upset, and what their experiences are with those who have a responsibility for their welfare.

We explore also the role of technology in online safeguarding and child protection and ask the question – is this always the best approach? Within this question there is much to unpick, starting from the role of technology in young people's lives and where the risks arise. We will define the broad issue of the impact of online technology on childhood – the opportunities – for example access to information, removal of geographical restrictions on interaction, social communication, entertainment, etc., but also the potential risks, like access to inappropriate or, to use the current policy buzzword, *harmful* content, the issue of being *always connected*, and the impact of screen time, unwanted attention and communication from those we may we to protect children from, opportunities to share and distribute self-generated materials, and the erosion of privacy.

To reflect on the requirements of code to achieve a safe digital child, we also, within this text, bring in much knowledge from other stakeholders in children's safeguarding. We work a great deal with other stakeholders in this area, with NGOs, charities, education and social care professionals, policy makers, and legal experts. This allows access to some data sets that will be drawn upon on throughout the course of this discussion, and enables observation of the stakeholder arena around online child safeguarding. This is something we have been doing for 15 years, and we now draw two major observations from this time:

1. Children and young people use a lot of online technology, it permeates all aspects of their lives, and, for the most part, they have a positive experience with it. The negative impacts rarely come from the technologies themselves, they come from how the technologies are used by others.
2. There are few people in the stakeholder space who aren't committed to the safeguarding of children and young people and who care passionately about ensuring they are *safe* and free of harm. All have opinions on how best to tackle the issues of *growing up in the digital age*. However, these opinions are rarely reinforced with a strong evidence base. As a discipline, online safeguarding is a young one – barely 20 years old. We are still finding our way and while the area is awash with policy documents, resources, and legislation, there is little in the way of hard evaluation of the impact of technologies and resources, and even less transparency in the implementation of technologies purported to safeguarding and protect children. While there are reasons this is completely acceptable – such as the protection of intellectual property and market position – it does make evaluation of the claims of the code highly problematic. And furthermore, this lack of evidence does little to prevent stakeholders thinking they know best and, of course, they all have the *solution* to online safeguarding.

What we *know*, from our work in this field, is that most of the problems come from social issues, and this is something we will focus upon in Chapter 2. While the digital networks might facilitate harm and conflict, they do not cause it – the humans on the edge of the network are the problem, not the code itself. As such, there is only so much one can achieve with a content and communications-based perspective rather than a behavioural-based perspective and there is a need for policy makers to understand this if the symbiosis between stakeholders is successful.

We would argue that there is a lack of understanding *in* the stakeholder space because that is a lack of understanding *of* the stakeholder space itself[9]. A stakeholder model for online child protection, which is an adaptation of the seminal work of Bronfenbrenner and his ecological framework of child development[10], is defined. Bronfenbrenner proposed an ecosystem of interconnections that facilitate the development of the child, and highlighted the different, and equally important, roles players in the system have. The important thing about Bronfenbrenner's work is that it clearly showed that there is no one independent entity that ensures the positive development of a child. It is cooperative systems and the interactions between them that result in healthy development. Perhaps most importantly in his model was the importance of mesosystems – the interactions between the different players in child development.

Arguably, this is something we have lost sight of in the online safeguarding world. By adapting this ecosystem for online safety, we can see both the breadth of stakeholder responsibilities for safeguarding, and how the stakeholders interact (see Figure 1.1).

The value of the model is that is shows the many different stakeholders in online safeguarding, and shows the importance of interactions (mesosystems) between them, as well as the distance a given stakeholder is from the child we wish to safeguard. There are many microsystems around the child, with whom the child directly interacts with, before we even approach the place of technology

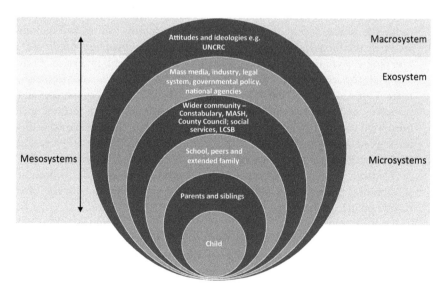

Figure 1.1 A stakeholder model for child online safety.

provides in this safeguarding model. If we are to consider the location of code, and algorithms, in this model, it is many steps beyond the child itself.

From the broad policy perspective, the focus of solution provision, and also social responsibility, it would seem, is entirely within the exosystem. And while we drive our expectations of responsibility at this layer, we lose focus on the roles in the microsystem, or the fact that encompassing all of this – the macrosystem – should be the rights of the child. Within this model, we have defined the UN Convention on the Rights of the Child[11] as the fundamental macrosystem around while the entire stakeholder space in enveloped. This should be any policy maker's go-to for the development of new resources, technologies, policy, or legislation. Yet this seems to be the most neglected, and often ignored, aspect of online child safeguarding. Arguably, it is sometimes viewed as a barrier for solutions, rather than the foundation of any legislative or policy development. However, in this text we will attempt to redress some of this balance – by establishing a rights-based framework against which different algorithmic approaches might be considered and evaluated.

While the nature of the debate around online child safeguarding is global, we do not have the space or time to draw upon the whole global picture. As such, we will focus upon the UK, as this is both the focus of much of our empirical work, and also a particularly active policy space around online safeguarding.

In April 2019 the UK Government has just released its "Online Harms" white paper[12]:

> The government wants the UK to be the safest place in the world to go online, and the best place to start and grow a digital business. Given the prevalence of illegal and harmful content online, and the level of public concern about online harms, not just in the UK but worldwide, we believe that the digital economy urgently needs a new regulatory framework to improve our citizens' safety online.
>
> Illegal and unacceptable content and activity is widespread online, and UK users are concerned about what they see and experience on the internet. The prevalence of the most serious illegal content and activity, which threatens our national security or the physical safety of children, is unacceptable. Online platforms can be a tool for abuse and bullying, and they can be used to undermine our democratic values and debate. The impact of harmful content and activity can be particularly damaging for children, and there are growing concerns about the potential impact on their mental health and wellbeing.

It continued:

> This White Paper sets out a programme of action to tackle content or activity that harms individual users, particularly children, or threatens our way of life in the UK, either by undermining national security, or by undermining our shared rights, responsibilities and opportunities to foster integration.

There is currently a range of regulatory and voluntary initiatives aimed at addressing these problems, but these have not gone far or fast enough, or been consistent enough between different companies, to keep UK users safe online … .

… The UK will be the first to do this, leading international efforts by setting a coherent, proportionate and effective approach that reflects our commitment to a free, open and secure internet.

As a world-leader in emerging technologies and innovative regulation, the UK is well placed to seize these opportunities. We want technology itself to be part of the solution, and we propose measures to boost the tech-safety sector in the UK, as well as measures to help users manage their safety online.

The UK has established a reputation for global leadership in advancing shared efforts to improve online safety. Tackling harmful content and activity online is one part of the UK's wider ambition to develop rules and norms for the internet, including protecting personal data, supporting competition in digital markets and promoting responsible digital design.

Perhaps the most telling comment from the opening pages of the white paper, however, come from the Ministerial introduction, that stated the paper formed part of the "UK's wider ambition to develop rules and norms for the internet". Harking back to John Perry Barlow's manifesto, is it really the UK government's place to develop rules and norms for the Internet? Of course we would expect them to provide the legislation to manage behaviours that might be facilitated online that affect their citizens, they surely cannot define *norms* for a global technology platform?

The white paper was a, arguably, logical conclusion to a policy direction that can be seen to take shape in 2012[13]. That direction focussed upon the use of technology to solve issues related to online child protection and safeguarding. The view being that given the online environment presents *risks* or *harms* (for example, access to inappropriate content such as pornography, access to harmful content that might relate to images of self-harm and suicide, abuse via messaging and chat platforms or the sharing of a self-generated indecent image on a minor) that might ultimately harm the child in some manner, the technology must also be able to provide the solution to prevent these things from happening. The focus in the early foundations of this policy direction was the prevention of access to pornographic content by children and young people. And the solution was seen to be filtering technologies, which would identify pornographic materials and prevent access.

From a human rights perspective, these pro-active filtering approaches have already attracted the concern of the United Nations, with the "Report of the Special Rapporteur on the promotion and protection of the right to freedom of opinion and expression" in 2018[14] stating that:

> States and intergovernmental organizations should refrain from establishing laws or arrangements that would require the 'proactive' monitoring or filtering of content, which is both inconsistent with the right to privacy and likely to amount to pre-publication censorship.

Nevertheless, there seems to be an increased focus on interceptional-content moderation from platform providers, and an expectation to monitor behaviour on these platforms in a more pro-active manner (with automated intervention), with the threat of legislation, should these calls not be heeded. This is a policy focus that began with young people's access to pornography, and the unacceptability of this but, as set out in the white paper, seems to have expanded greatly to all manner of *harms*. Even though the one area that has an established progression from policy to legislation has yet to show evidence of success.

In considering how we got to this point in the policy space, it is useful to look at its origins, which emerged in the UK with an All-Party Inquiry into Child Online Safety in 2012[15] which was the catalyst to a speech made in 2013, by the then British Prime Minister David Cameron[16]. In this speech Mr Cameron stated:

> I want to talk about the internet, the impact it's having on the innocence of our children, how online pornography is corroding childhood and how, in the darkest corners of the internet, there are things going on that are a direct danger to our children and that must be stamped out.

Mr Cameron continued with proposals how to tackle each problem. Firstly, tackling child abuse images online:

> You're the people who have worked out how to map almost every inch of the earth from space who have developed algorithms that make sense of vast quantities of information. You're the people who take pride in doing what they say can't be done. You hold hackathons for people to solve impossible internet conundrums. Well – hold a hackathon for child safety. Set your greatest brains to work on this. You are not separate from our society, you are part of our society, and you must play a responsible role in it.

And for tackling youth access to online pornography:

> By the end of this year, when someone sets up a new broadband account the settings to install family friendly filters will be automatically selected. If you just click 'next' or 'enter', then the filters are automatically on. And, in a really big step forward, all the ISPs have rewired their technology so that once your filters are installed, they will cover any device connected to your home internet account. No more hassle of downloading filters for every device, just one click protection. One click to protect your whole home and keep your children safe.

We will explore the approaches to filtering and content control in far more detail in Chapter 3 as well as considering in more detail the policy around this approach to online safeguarding. The reason we explore it here is because we can see, from both David Cameron's speech and also the Online Harms white paper that the focus remains one where technology needs to provide the solutions to these *technological problems*. As this ideology progressed, we saw many examples of the view that technology could tackle all manner of online social issues, centring around technology companies providing *solutions* to ensure children are safe from the variety of risks associated with going online. For example, in recent years we have had a number of calls, such as:

- The Health secretary calling for algorithms to be installed onto children's mobile phones to detect indecent images and prevent them from being sent[17, 18]
- Legislation to impose age verification technology on anyone wishing to access pornography from a UK based device[19]
- Calls to extend age verification onto social media sites to ensure no-one under 13 can access these services and for social media companies to ensure children cannot access their services for more than two hours per day[20]
- Calls for social media companies to stop the live streaming of terrorist activities[21]
- Calls for social media companies to prevent the posting of "anti-vax" materials[22]

Yet for those of us with a knowledge on the capabilities of code we have known for a long time that technology can only ever be a tool to support the broader social context of these issues.

There are some things that digital technology is very good at in this area. It can:

- Provide reporting routes and provide responsive, and transparent, takedowns
- Provide warnings about content based on keyword analysis and, in some cases, image comparison
- Pre-screen content that is easily identifiable because it has been previously classified
- Monitor network access and raise alerts using rule-based systems, for example, on a known website that provides access to harmful content
- Provide the means to block abusers
- Interpret new data based upon its similarity to previous data that has been shown

However, there are other things that technology is far less efficient at:

- Detecting the inference of context in textual content
- Identifying content outside of clearly defined heuristics
- Image processing in a broad and subjective context (for example "indecency")
- Subjective interpretation of meaning and nuance in textual data

Digital technology is very good at clearly defined, rule-based functionality in easily contained system boundaries. Or, to put it another way, data processing, analysis, and pattern matching of data. Computers are very good at taking data and analysing it based upon rules defined within the system (for example, identify words that *might* relate to sexual content). As we will explore in later chapters in this text, what they are far less efficient at are interpretation, *intelligence*, and inference.

By way of an illustrative, albeit trivial, example, let us take the word "cock". This is a term that might be related to a sexual context – it could refer colloquially to male genitalia. Equally, it might refer to an animal. If we consider this from the perspective of a filtering system, that might be tasked with ensuring an end user cannot access websites of a sexual nature, we might provide that system with a list of keywords that could indicate sexual content. "Cock" may be one of these terms. The filtering system will be very good at pattern matching this string of characters to any mentioned within any given website and will successfully "block" access to this content. However, it will be far less efficient at determining the actual context of the website – it *might* be about sexual activity; however, it might also be about animal husbandry. While there are techniques, discussed in more detail in Chapter 3, that might allow the filter to make a more nuanced guess, such as considering other words around the term "cock", it cannot be certain.

Even with this simple example, we can see how it might struggle to prevent access to all sexual content or, equally, result in *false positives* – blocking innocuous[23] sites that are not "inappropriate" for children to see (also referred to as overblocking). Given the policy direction, and the pressure exacted upon service providers as a result, it is likely that algorithms will be implemented to be conservative in their filtering – worrying less about overblocking and more at ensuring as much sexual content as possible is captured. A simple and popular example of this comes from the overblocking of the Northern English town of Scunthorpe[24], given that a substring of its composition is a vulgar word for female genitalia.

This book considers the role of technology in online safeguarding and protection and warns that we may be moving toward a *safeguarding dystopia* through an overreliance on technical solutions that are not effective, accurate, or proportionate how they resolve safeguarding issues.

We can also illustrate the disparity this focus of expecting technology providers to *do more* causes by drawing upon a couple of simple examples.

The first example highlights how technology can be used in a safeguarding context, directed from legislation, in a manner that ends up in something of a nonsense. It also illustrates that safeguarding technology that might be viable and a useful tool, also needs to be supported with clear policy and practice around its use. In this case that occurred in the UK in 2016, a teenaged boy was accused of being radicalised as a result of accessing the UK Independence Party's website in his school[25]. According to news reports, the school monitoring systems detected that the boy had accessed the website that had been flagged as potential evidence of radicalisation. Since 2015, schools have had a statutory responsibility to monitor potential risks of radicalisation in their student population, as part of their *Prevent duty*[26], including aspects of online sources that might allude to evidence of radicalised behaviours or have been identified as a site providing access to radicalisation materials. Failure to carry out these duties could result in safeguarding inspection or fines for the school. Therefore, it is little surprise that when a monitoring system triggers an alert related to radicalisation, the school will bring in the police. However, it seems somewhat concerning, from the rights of the child under article 17 of the CRC (*children and young people should be able to access information, particularly from the media*), that accessing a mainstream political party's website triggers such an alert. While reporting on the story is, by its nature, always somewhat incomplete and may be subject to bias, we know from our work in schools that in a lot of cases schools are concerns about what to do with monitoring reports, and whether police intervention is always necessary. Put another way – they are expected to put technology in place, without any guidance on using it sensibly within a clear incident response framework. The policy and legislative aspects to these concerns centre upon, in this case, the need for technology to be in place (this is explored in more detail in Chapter 3) as if this, and this alone, is a safeguarding solution.

The responsibility of the service providers to *do more* and to expect technological solutions to what are essentially technological facilitated social problems is rife in the online safeguarding space, and can frequently cause tension between the technology providers and the policy makers (as has been the case with the launch of the online harms white paper[27]). Within this text, while we argue strongly that technology is not *the* solution to online safeguarding and child protection, we are not saying that technology does not have a role to play. We are, however, stating the technology should be used within the limits of effectiveness, working with the strengths digital technology and information processing brings, without placing unrealistic expectations based upon poorly defined requirements and misunderstood capabilities.

An excellent example of a case of a service provider being able to *do more* within realistic technological expectations comes from a case from Belfast, Northern Ireland[28] that was played out in the last couple of years and settled in early 2018. In this case, a Belfast teenager took out litigation against Facebook as a result of repeated sharing of indecent images of her, as a 14-year-old, on a *shame* page on the platform. While she had repeatedly had these images reported and taken down, the images were reposted several times. Her view was that Facebook's failure to prevent these images being reposted was a misuse of information pertaining to herself, and therefore negligence. While Facebook had resisted the claim, it was eventually admitted as a class action and ended as an out of court settlement.

This case is significant because the logic behind the litigation was sound – if a platform provider has seen a reported image and made a judgement to take down that image because it breaches community standards, presents copyright issues with which the provider does not wish to become embroiled in, or that the image was clearly illegal (as would be the case with an indecent image of a 14-year-old) then the technology exists to be able to "fingerprint" that image and check any subsequent uploading of images to see if an attempt is made to post it again. We will explore this fingerprinting technology in more detail in subsequent chapters, but the core principle (referred to as hashing[29]) is applying an algorithm to the data in the image to create a unique identifying token (analogous to a fingerprint) such that any time the same process is applied to the same set of data (which is in essence what an image is – it is a set of data related to pixels of different colours in a grid-based layout), the same token will be created. Therefore, it could be quite rightly argued if a user has taken the time to report an image and the platform moderators have agreed that the image should be taken down, it is perfectly possible to hash this image and intercept any further attempts to post. Failure to do this, as the litigation argued, would be negligent and an abuse of an individual's personal data. It is interesting to note that while the settlement of the case is private, Facebook has announced a similar approach to tackling revenge pornography posts since the case[30].

This case highlights the role technology *can* play in safeguarding, and how it can be applied in a sensible and responsible manner, doing what technology is very good at doing (data processing and repetitive tasks). It also highlights that technology can be applied in a manner that is cognisant of the rights of the child.

As we have already discussed, there is a risk in our rush to safeguarding and protecting young people from the "darkest corners of the Internet". There is a risk if we adopt approaches that do not consider their rights and, in some cases, erode them. Without having children's rights at the centre of any online safeguarding solution we would argue that these "solutions" are utterly counterproductive as we are anticipating children and young people accepting an erosion of their rights in order to keep them safe and secure. And this can, as we will discuss in later chapters, have knock-on impacts into their adult lives.

While there have been attempts to define *digital rights*[31], we would argue that there is no need for new rights, given we have a well-established and ratified set of children's rights in the UN Convention on the Rights of the Child (UN CRC)[32], "the most rapidly and widely ratified international human rights treaty in history". While this is clearly a convention, rather than legislation, it does provide a valid, thought-provoking, and often neglected acknowledgement that children and young people are entitled to human rights and it is the role of stakeholders in their welfare, such as parents and governments, to ensure these rights are protected.

In developing arguments in this text, particularly when considering the role of technology in safeguarding, it is important to consider safeguarding approaches against the rights of the child. With this in mind, as we draw this opening chapter to a close, we define a framework that is useful when evaluating these different approaches. Drawing from the UN CRC, this framework allows us to apply a uniform and critical approach to the evaluation of different technologies using an approach that places the child at the centre of the analysis, considers their human rights and how the algorithms have a positive or negative impact on these. Table 1.1 defines the framework as a series of rights we consider to be applicable to the safeguarding and online space, as well as a rationale for their inclusion.

The remainder of this book explores in more detail how technologies might be useful in online child safeguarding and where they will be less effective, and how they impact upon children's rights. As a starting point for this, the next

Table 1.1 A rights-based framework to assess the impact of safeguarding technologies

Article 3 – best interests of the child	There is potential for technology to be applied to safeguarding scenarios that might negatively impact upon the wellbeing and rights of the child
Article 8 – protection and preservation of identity	Technology may potentially be implemented to share the child's identity, or part of their identity, in an unlawful or unethical manner
Article 12 – respect for the views of the child	Technological tools might, in order to ensure their safety, limit how these views may be expressed online
Article 13 – freedom of expression	Technological tools might, in order to ensure their safety, limit this expression and also control access to information that might support this expression
Article 15 – freedom of association	Technology may limit young people's access to participation in entirely valid online associations
Article 16 – the right to privacy	Technology may erode a child's privacy (for example through excessive monitoring) while attempting to ensure their safety
Article 17 – access to information from the media	When technology is implemented to control access to certain kinds of harmful content, it might inadvertently prevent access to legitimate media sources
Article 28 – the right to education	Technologies that prevent access to certain types of harmful content might also block access to information relevant to a child's education (for example, information related to healthy sexual relationships)
Article 29 – the goals of education	Specifically "The preparation of the child for responsible life in a free society" – if, through technological safeguarding, a child has limited access to educational resources that make them aware of equality, health issues and rights, there is a risk the goals of education will not be met

chapter begins by reviewing, against a large dataset and some secondary sources, the nature of harm as reported by young people, and how their internet access is managed in the home. This allows us to reflect upon what young people tell us upsets them, compared to what algorithms attempt to protect them against, and also whether the policy direction is actually pointing the right way.

The succeeding chapters will then develop an analysis of different technologies purported to safeguarding against online risk in some way, alongside the rationale and policy perspectives in their development and deployment, against the right framework defined previously. The book begins by exploring the most well-established technologies such as filtering and monitoring, before exploring more specifically the control to access to pornography in more detail. It will then explore more leading-edge technologies, such as those that might employ algorithmic techniques and *artificial intelligence* approaches for image recognition or behavioural analysis. The book will draw to a close by critically appraising the algorithmic approaches used in online safeguarding and child safety, to reflect upon whether these technologies, in the main, have a positive impact or whether we are, through an overreliance on technology and expectations that technology can tackle any potential harm or abuse in the online safeguarding space, moving ever closer towards the *safeguarding dystopia*, which attempts to protect children while systematically disregarding their rights, attempting to control them and make them docile, and impacting negatively on their wellbeing. All of which occurs when we try to achieve an impossible goal – to ensure every time a child goes online they will be safe and entirely risk-free.

Notes

1 Perry Barlow, John (1996). "Declaration of Independence for Cyberspace". www.eff.org/cyberspace-independence
2 FCC (1996). "Telecommunications Act of 1996". www.fcc.gov/general/tele-communications-act-1996
3 Cheswick, W. R., Bellovin, S. M. and Rubin, A. D. (2003). Firewalls and Internet Security: Repelling the Wily Hacker. Boston, MA: Addison-Wesley Professional. p. 202.
4 Phippen, A. (2017). *Children's Online Behaviour and Safety – Policy and Rights Challenges*. London: Palgrave MacMillan.
5 Lessig, Lawrence (2006). "Code Is Law / Code 2.0". www.socialtext.net/codev2/code_is_law
6 While we acknowledge that digital technology also relies on hardware – communication networks and physical devices – they are essentially non-functioning collections of wires and rare earth metals without the code to make anything happen.
7 UK Government (2017). "The Digital Economy Act 2017 Part 3". www.legislation.gov.uk/ukpga/2017/30/part/3/enacted
8 Reidenberg, J. (1997), "Lex Informatica: The formulation of information policy rules through technology", *Texas Law Review*, 553.
9 Bond, E. and Phippen, A. (2019). "Why is placing the child at the centre of online safeguarding so difficult?". *Ent. L.R.*, 30(3).
10 Bronfenbrenner, U. (1979). The Ecology of Human Development: Experiments by Nature and Design. Cambridge, MA: Harvard University Press.
11 United Nations (1989). "Convention on the Rights of the Child". www.ohchr.org/Documents/ProfessionalInterest/crc.pdf
12 UK Government (2019). "Online Harms White Paper". https://assets.publishing.service.gov.uk/government/uploads/system/uploads/attachment_data/file/793360/Online_Harms_White_Paper.pdf
13 Phippen, A. (2017). *Children's Online Behaviour and Safety – Policy and Rights Challenges*. London: Palgrave MacMillan.
14 United Nations Human Rights Council (2018). "Report of the Special Rapporteur on the promotion and protection of the right to freedom of opinion and expression". https://documents-dds-ny.un.org/doc/UNDOC/GEN/G18/096/72/PDF/G1809672.pdf?OpenElement
15 Independent Parliamentary Inquiry into Online Child Protection (2012). "Findings and Recommendations". www.safermedia.org.uk/Images/final-report.pdf
16 UK Government (2013). "The Internet and Pornography: Prime Minister calls for Action".www.gov.uk/government/speeches/the-internet-and-pornography-prime-minister-calls-for-action

17 House of Commons Science and Technology Committee (2017). "Impact of Social Media and Screen-use on Young People's Health". https://publications.parliament.uk/pa/cm201719/cmselect/cmsctech/822/822.pdf

18 This statement is actually a useful proposal with which to deconstruct arguments around image recognition being used for the automatic detection of indecent images and therefore is discussed in far greater detail in Chapter 5.

19 UK Government (2017). "The Digital Economy Act 2017 Part 3". www.legislation.gov.uk/ukpga/2017/30/part/3/enacted

20 Helm, T. and Rawnsley, A. (2018). "Health Chiefs to Set Social Media Time Limits for Young People".www.theguardian.com/media/2018/sep/29/health-chief-set-social-media-time-limits-young-people

21 BBC News (2019). "Christchurch Shootings: Sajid Javid Warns Tech Giants over Footage". www.bbc.co.uk/news/uk-47593536

22 Mohdin, A. (2019). "Matt Hancock 'Won't Rule Out' Compulsory Vaccinations". www.theguardian.com/politics/2019/may/04/matt-hancock-wont-rule-out-compulsory-vaccinations

23 We will use the term "innocuous" sites to describe those who have been incorrectly blocked based upon the requirements of the filter (for example, pornography, gambling, drugs and alcohol) and not "legal", because access to pornography is legal in the UK.

24 Wikipedia (n.d.). "The Scunthorpe Problem". https://en.wikipedia.org/wiki/Scunthorpe_problem

25 Gutteridge, N. (2016). "PC gone mad: Outrage as school calls police after pupil looks at Ukip website in class". www.express.co.uk/news/uk/647539/Ukip-UK-Independence-Party-school-police-called-website

26 UK Department for Education (2015). "The Prevent duty – Departmental advice for schools and childcare providers". https://assets.publishing.service.gov.uk/government/uploads/system/uploads/attachment_data/file/439598/prevent-duty-departmental-advice-v6.pdf

27 Martineua, P (2019). "The UK's Tech Backlash Could Change the Internet". www.wired.com/story/uk-tech-backlash-could-change-internet/

28 Irwin, A. (2018). "Girl (14) Settles Landmark Action against Facebook over Naked Images". www.irishtimes.com/news/crime-and-law/courts/high-court/girl-14-settles-landmark-action-against-facebook-over-naked-images-1.3349974

29 Venkatesan, R., Koon, S. M., Jakubowski, M. H. and Moulin, P. (2000). Robust image hashing. In Proceedings 2000 International Conference on Image Processing (Cat. No. 00CH37101) (Vol. 3, pp. 664–666). IEEE.

30 Davis, A. (2018)" The Facts: Non-Consensual Intimate Image Pilot". https://newsroom.fb.com/news/h/non-consensual-intimate-image-pilot-the-facts/

31 5Rights Foundation (2019). "The 5Rights". https://5rightsfoundation.com/the-5-rights/

32 United Nations (1989). "Convention on the Rights of the Child". www.ohchr.org/Documents/ProfessionalInterest/crc.pdf

2 The role of online technology in young people's lives
Activities and concerns

In this chapter we consider those at the centre of the safeguarding scenario – children and young people. We do this in order that we better understand what their online usage comprises, and why technological solutions to safeguarding will sometimes not be sufficient to ensure their risk-free use of technology. Specifically, it explores primary data collected from our work with an online safety charity – SWGfL[1] – who have, for a number of years, run a survey with school children to explore how and why they go online, what their concerns and views on online harm are, and how they engage in the family setting around safeguarding measures. This is a useful starting point for this text because it allows us to bring a youth perspective to the analysis of the technical approaches used to *ensure* their safety. We will also, in part, draw on other complementary research on young people's online behaviours and safeguards.

The SWGfL survey tool was constructed to collect basic information on:

- online usage (devices, kinds of activity, time online)
- upsetting content (both frequency and type of upset)
- issues related to abuse (saying or receiving abusive comments)
- the sorts of things that cause upset online
- views related to online safety and wellbeing
- controls of their internet use

For the purposes of this analysis, we will focus on usage, upsetting content, and controls on their internet use (as an interesting reflection on whether home-based safeguarding measures are effective). We will also consider some differences in response according to the age of the respondents, as the survey collects data from both primary and secondary school children.

The survey was initially piloted with a primary and secondary school to determine the effectiveness and how understandable the questions were. While there were early revisions to the survey, it was launched in October 2012 and has had a stable question set since then. While there have been new questions added since inception, none have been modified or taken away.

Since launch, we have collected responses from over 20,000 children and young people from over 100 schools. The survey[2] is disseminated to school partners by

SWGfL, and the schools administer the survey in class so a broad cross-section of respondents is reached. Since the commencement of the latest version of the survey in February 2016 we have collected data from 9,285 responses and it is from these responses that we present some baselines regarding what young people say concerns them around online harms, and where technology is being used as an intervention in home settings.

Basic demographics for the survey show a fairly equal split of male and female respondents and while we will not dwell too heavily on gender differences, it is useful to know this equal split (see Table 2.1).

The spread of ages is also broad[3] and we will explore some differences in ages in the presentation of this data. Moreover, given the small comparable numbers we have for Year 12 and 13, we will not be considering those in detail (see Table 2.2).

We also ask some basic statistics about technology use and application. Clearly, from the results in table 3 and 4, we have a technologically engaged population who use online technologies for a number of different reasons (see Table 2.3 and Table 2.4).

Table 2.1 Respondent gender

Male	48.83%
Female	51.17%

Table 2.2 What year group are you in?

Year 4	13.88%
Year 5	17.01%
Year 6	18.86%
Year 7	12.58%
Year 8	10.8%
Year 9	8.65%
Year 10	6.5%
Year 11	6.41%
Year 12	2.65%
Year 13	2.64%

Table 2.3 How much time do you spend online in an average day?

Less than an hour	24.25%
One to three hours	42.44%
Between three and six hours	22.58%
More than six hours	10.73%

Table 2.4 What do you use the internet for?

Social networks	50.60%
Messaging	43.08%
Gaming	67.30%
Shopping	35.90%
News	25.50%
Browsing/general entertainment	46.79%
Listening to music	70.57%
Uploading/content creation (e.g. making YouTube videos)	27.52%

However, the focus of this analysis lies in what young people report as upsetting in order to juxtapose against technological approaches which are, in general, designed and put in place to ensure they aren't harmed while going online. While some people might argue that some technologies associated more explicitly with child protection (such as image recognition to identify abused children) fall outside of this broad and generalized definition, the majority of classes of safeguarding technology (filtering, monitoring, tracking) usually follow a harm-reduction rationale. We should also note that the responses would highlight that young people do not merely consume content online, they communicate with it using social media and messaging, and are, in significant numbers (almost 28%) creating and contributing their own content.

The proportion of our respondents who said that they had seen things online that have upset them is significant, albeit in the minority. Overall around a third across the whole population said they had been upset by something they had seen online (see Table 2.5).

Unsurprisingly, if we break this response down with ages, the older the respondent, the more likely (in general) they are to have experienced upset online (see Table 2.6).

Perhaps unsurprisingly, once our respondents are at secondary age the likelihood of seeing upsetting things online increases significantly. Up until year 7 the proportion is just below 30%, with a little variation per year. However, there is a year on year increase from year 8 onwards.

One of the most interesting aspects of this analysis, given the theme of this text, is to explore the nature of what young people report as being upsetting online – for example, are they upset in general by the behaviour of others or from the content they are seeing? While there seems to be a belief from the Online

Table 2.5 Have you ever seen anything online
            that has made you feel upset?

Yes	32.03%
No	67.97%

Table 2.6 Have you ever seen anything online that has made
you feel upset? Age differences

	Yes	*No*
Year 4	28.30%	71.70%
Year 5	25.82%	74.18%
Year 6	28.98%	71.02%
Year 7	25.95%	74.05%
Year 8	31.41%	68.59%
Year 9	40.87%	59.13%
Year 10	40.99%	59.01%
Year 11	48.01%	51.99%

Harms white paper that the majority of harms come from specific types of content (for example, pornography, terrorist material, self-harm and suicide images), and therefore safeguarding approaches should adopt a prohibitive approach to ensure these harmful types of content should not be seen, what young people report in this survey would suggest this is perhaps not reflected in their experiences.

We ask a supplementary question to "Have you ever seen anything on line that has made you feel upset?" which requests for them to explain what they have seen that was upsetting. Using word clouds to illustrate the responses, we can see the key themes that emerge (see Figure 2.1).

The predominant responses seem to be "people" and "news". While video, an indication of upset by content, is also significant in the word cloud that there seems to be a higher probability that human interaction is the cause of the upset, or content from news media, rather than what might be classified at a policy level as "harmful". This presents challenges from technology, given that news filtering might be considered to be censorship, given the already stringent controls over broadcast news – even if young people are reporting that news coverage is upsetting, it would be a challenging policy decision to decide the best way to protect them is to prohibit them from seeing it. It would also be challenged by Article 17 of the UN CRC. Equally, if interactions with others ("people" or "someone") are the cause of upset, we could consider approaches that would prevent interaction, but this would be unjustifiably controlling and challenge Article 15 of the UN CRC.

By way of further example, we have drawn a number of specific examples, that illustrate the breadth of upset, even when we attempt to categorise across the whole data set.[4] These quotes are taken directly from responses, with no editing and, while sometimes shocking, are an authentic representation of a youth voice (see Table 2.7)[5].

We can see, from this simple overview of reported harmful experience that, similarly to the word cloud, a lot of harms arise not from the content of itself, but from the behaviour of others, using the platforms to abuse or upset.

Figure 2.1 Would you like to explain what it was that upset you?

This presents a safeguarding challenge if we are to adopt algorithmic approaches to solving these issues. While algorithms are very good at precise, well specified logical flow (for example "identify words from the following set and prevent content containing these words from being displayed") they are far less effective at interpretive identification of behavioural or nuanced communication, such as "using the words in this set, make a decision on whether the recipient of these words is being abused".

We will return to this issue when exploring the algorithmic and technical approaches both implemented and proposed in online child safeguarding and protection policy. However, it is worthwhile to reflect upon in this part of the text as it provides a baseline of what young people report what is causing them upset and, therefore, one would hope is evidence is the foundation of policy forming, should be the focus of any technical countermeasures to these harms.

A final aspect of the exploration of this large dataset draws from an appreciation of the type of environment with which our young people engage with online technologies at home, and how parents attempt to ensure "protection

Table 2.7 Examples of upsetting content, as expressed by young people

1. Abuse – Abusive comments directed at the respondent by others
   - I was told to suck my mum and fuck my dad and I was a nigga (KS2)
   - Some kid called Denzel said he is going to find where I live and kill me (KS2)
2. Animal cruelty – Content related to the abuse of animals
   - Sad dogs being rescued and I cried because of the condition they were in (YouTube) (KS2)
   - Yulin Fesival (KS3)
3. Bystander – Observation of abusive comments directed toward others
   - I haven't been bullied but a lot of people I know have and couldn't tell anyone (KS3)
   - People being horrible to a little girl called <redacted> rose as she is disabled and smaller than a normal person (KS3)
4. Gaming – Upset caused by behaviours in gaming, for example 'griefing', damage to environments in games, etc.
   - A guy destroying my bridge on a game (KS2)
   - On a game someone Admin Abused[a] me (KS3)
5. Grooming – Comments directed at the recipient asking them questions related to themselves, (age, sex, location, etc.)
   - A person lied about who they are and tried to meet up and have a relationship when I did not know them (KS2)
   - Proud pedophiles (sic.)/"MAPs"[b] on social media normally used by minors (KS4)
6. Hacking – Incidents of hacking, malware, etc.
   - I was on my far-out game and I was almost hacked and I lost the game forever (KS2)
   - Someone hacked into a friends account and posted her information online (KS4)
7. Homophobia – Homophobic comments and content
   - People bullying a gay person (KS3)
8. News and media – Upset caused by content from news media, advertising, etc.
   - Bradley Lowery's death (KS3)[c]
   - A Muslim lady was stabbed on a train and I take the train every day so that frightened me (KS3)[d]
9. 9 Offline related issue – Upset related to something that occurs in an offline context, for example, involving friends/family members
   - I've seen my sister online and I don't see her (KS2)
10. Peer behaviour – Observations of the behaviour of others in friendship groups and of similar age
    - People getting drunk/wasted at a party when they were only 15/16 (KS4)
    - I've been upset by how cutting people can be when you don't see eye to eye on a subject (KS4)
11. Pornography – Sexually explicit content
    - Even with child filters on a lot can seep through and you can see some pretty disturbing things you can never unsee (KS4)
    - I saw Peppa Pig "doing it" with a horse and the horse tore right through poor old Peppa (KS4)[e]
12. Racism – Content or comment that is racist
    - People being racist to black people (KS2)
    - Someone saying I don't have friends because I'm black skin colour (KS2)
13. Scary content – Content intended to scare the recipient, for example, horror movies and certain types of games (e.g. SlenderMan)
    - I was watching a video with my friend in year 7 and we watched a scary video (KS2)
    - Pictures of ghost and others scary tales (KS3)
    - Scary pictures of clowns (KS3)
14. Swearing – Comments containing profanity
    - They where using rude words (KS2)
15. Upsetting content – Content that the respondent discloses has caused them upset
    - Logan Paul video when he put the video of someone who hung himself and then he laughed (KS2)
    - A person cut in half called Daliha and she was found in the country side and now I dont like going to see my grandma because she lives in the country side but my mum says its not true (KS2)[f]
    - One of my emails said would you like to f*ck with me and it was scary and creepy. I also have got a lot of spam about fitness pills (KS3)
16. Violent content – For example violence in movies, terrorist content, some explicit content in gaming
    - It was someone getting their heart cut out (KS2)
    - I have seen beheadings and suicides mostly (KS4)

[a] Admin Abuse is as aspect of multi player gaming where a player with admin level privileges makes use of this to penalise or punish other players without any way for those players to respond.

[b] Minor Attracted Person.

[c] Similarly, in July 2017, following the death of Bradley Lowry, there were a number of responses talking about this.

[d] This is evidence of a respondent relating, due to some commonality of everyday life, the content to their own lived experiences, in this case being scared to take a train because they saw a news story of someone being murdered on a train.

[e] The descriptions of pornographic content for KS4 respondents was generally far more graphic and extreme than for those of younger age.

[f] This relates to the murder of Elizabeth Short, who was murdered and mutilated in 1947 and was the subject of a 2006 movie. In this case it is not clear what the respondent has seen but they relate it to their own experiences of visiting their grandmother in the countryside.

from harm" in the home. The quotes are deliberate, because as we will highlight later in this discussion, perhaps parental perspectives on harm are equally distorted compared to what young people tell us.

Firstly, we ask whether there are "house rules" that young people are subject to in order that there might be some level of safeguarding in the home. Unsurprisingly, the majority of respondents said that there were (see Table 2.8).

However, we can also see that just over a third of respondents state that they do not have any controls or safeguards in the home. When asked what these safeguards are, we have a broad range (see Table 2.9).

Many of these would have a level of technical intervention with them, for example access control, time limits, site monitoring, and age restriction. Others could have a technical element but equally they might be rule-based safeguards that are imposed by parents and enacted in the family unit. If we consider the age of the respondent and the type of safeguards, we see some variation (see Table 2.10).

We can see with these responses that rules and safeguards in general tend to reduce when young people get older, which somewhat contrasts with what young people tell us about the high likelihood of seeing or experiencing upset online as they grow older. It is not a surprise that "Not allowed online after a certain time in the evening" increases as young people get older – it is unlikely younger children would be awake to have this rule applied. We also see that still frequently extolled rule around "only allow them online in a family room" is something of a myth, as one might expect given the number of opportunities in a modern household that a young person might be able to go online (laptops, PCs, tablets, mobile devices, gaming consoles). While it is interesting to note the sort of rules that are applied to young people in the home, what is more interesting, given our wish to explore *effective* approaches to online safeguarding and child protection in this text, is whether young people tell us it is possible to "get around" these rules. We will return to this issue in more detail in subsequent chapters, but we

Table 2.8 Are there any rules at home for using the internet?

Yes	65.73%
No	34.27%

Table 2.9 If yes, what sort of rules are there? (Please tick all that apply)

Parents control access to sites I can visit	38.60%
Ages restrictions on Internet access	37.24%
Parents can see what I look at online	47.53%
Only allowed online for a certain amount of time	48.91%
Not allowed online after a certain time in the evening	51.38%
Only allowed to go online in family rooms eg living room/kitchen	15.21%

Table 2.10 If yes, what sort of rules are there? (Please tick all that apply) – Age differences

	Parents control access to sites I can visit	Ages restrictions on Internet access	Parents can see what I look at online	Only allowed online for a certain amount of time	Not allowed online after a certain time in the evening	Only allowed to go online in family rooms eg living room/kitchen
Year 4	44.11%	32.66%	55.25%	53.45%	48.14%	20.25%
Year 5	42.47%	40.21%	54.83%	53.52%	49.70%	16.54%
Year 6	41.06%	41.13%	52.64%	50.12%	51.46%	13.95%
Year 7	35.64%	39.82%	48.04%	47.91%	51.04%	12.40%
Year 8	32.76%	38.77%	37.91%	43.74%	53.69%	13.38%
Year 9	29.75%	32.75%	30.50%	38.00%	55.75%	10.75%
Year 10	26.52%	29.55%	23.48%	41.67%	60.61%	9.09%
Year 11	22.78%	23.33%	21.11%	37.22%	62.22%	9.44%

Table 2.11 If you answered yes to rules at home, do you know how to get around these restrictions?

Yes	27.33%
No	39.26%
Some of them	33.40%

know[6] that sometimes technical measures put in place to "protect" young people are ineffective. Unsurprisingly, our young respondents tell us that the majority of them are capable of bypassing at least some of the house rules (see Table 2.11).

And equally unsurprisingly, as young people get older, they become more capable of bypassing rules see Table 2.12).

While the number of young people who report they are not capable of circumvention remains relatively static, the amount who are clear that they are capable of bypassing all rules increased significantly as they become teenagers.

In contrasting attitudes of young people to that of parents, we can reflect a great deal on the parent's sessions carried out in schools and the discussions therein, but also a further piece of survey work that draws from a separate survey conducted by Mumsnet and the Internet Watch Foundation[7], to which we provided some input around parental controls, that aimed to gain a detailed parental perspective on concerns and how they manage them.

Firstly, in reflecting upon many discussions with parents in educative settings, we can observe that there is not a "typical" parent in this scenario. Some will place great faith in technological solutions and believe that with technology in place to prevent harm, there requires no further intervention. For others, a more

Table 2.12 If you answered yes to rules at home, do you know how to get around these restrictions? Age differences

	Yes	*Some of them*	*No*
Year 4	28.22%	36.64%	35.14%
Year 5	26.70%	36.65%	36.65%
Year 6	24.74%	34.77%	40.49%
Year 7	24.36%	34.77%	40.86%
Year 8	23.40%	30.67%	45.93%
Year 9	33.05%	28.45%	38.49%
Year 10	36.94%	28.23%	34.83%
Year 11	40.91%	21.90%	37.19%

hands-on approach to *digital parenting* means that they are more likely to physically monitor their children's online and play a more active role in ensuring safety from harm. Of course, there are others that fall between these two modes of parenting. In drawing upon the data from the Mumsnet survey, we can see two contrasting issues – firstly the type of concerns they have, and also their confidence in dealing with them.

The data draws from research which analysed the parents data that was conducted as part of a joint study between SWGfL, the Office of the Australian eSafety Commissioner, and Netsafe New Zealand exploring parental attitudes toward pornography and was presented in a report comparing cultural differences[8]. While there is more detailed reporting of the findings in that report, there are a number of useful pieces of data that support our exploration here.

The first set of data that is relevant to this study relates to parental concerns – parents were presented with a number of different online "risks" and asked to state which ones concerned them. We can see from Table 2.13 that a content-based risk is one that is a greater concern than others, specifically pornography.

Table 2.13 Parental concerns

Being exposed to sexual imagery/pornography	78%
Bullying	76%
Being exposed to unpleasant or aggressive people (eg trolls, bad language)	76%
Being exposed to violent imagery	74%
Grooming	69%
Child sexual exploitation via video or photographs	63%
Making arrangements to meet strangers in real life	63%
Issues to do with body image and self esteem	63%
Internet use interfering with sleeping patterns	53%
Being exposed to extremist attitudes	52%
Internet use interfering with other hobbies and interests	46%
Internet use interfering with homework	41%

In contrast, pornography is rarely reported in our young people's survey as a concern for getting upset online. While this might not be surprising – given that many young people would not consider viewing pornography as particularly problematic. However, we would argue that young people report a far broader set of concerns, whereas adult stakeholders with safeguarding responsibilities seem to have pornography as a focus. We might observe, given the political and media narrative over recent years, that pornography is a concern because they are told this is something they should be worried about, and this is something we will develop in Chapter 3. In general, there are a wide range of concerns, from content-based issues to those related to contact and also behaviour among peer groups. Therefore, it is interesting, given this broad range of issues, to consider the popularity of different safeguarding approaches (see Table 2.14).

With this data we can see similarities in what is reported by young people, although the high statistic around "We can see what the children look at" might suggest some level of covert monitoring, rather than something the children are aware of. This is not something we can unpick from the data but, again, something we will return to later in this text. We can also see that there is a significant reliance on digital technology (filtering and monitoring) to manage online lives in the home. We can also compare these responses with the UK Communications Regulator's (OFCOM) recently released 2018 Media Literacy report[9] which stated that around 56% of parents they surveyed used at least one technical tool to manage their children's Internet access.

However, drawing upon the OFCOM research, we see one of the biggest differences between parental attitudes and that of young people. In the OFCOM research they stated that 15% of parents of 5–15-year-olds believed their children could circumvent ISP-level filtering and 10% could get around parental control software. Given what young people report to us, we might consider this statistic, in reality, to be far higher.

In this chapter we have considered what young people tell us they consider upsetting and harmful online, along with reporting on how house rules are implemented at home, and whether they might be able to circumvent them. It is unquestionable that young people as a whole are highly engaged with digital technology now, and use online services for a variety of reasons. And they report

Table 2.14 Parent online safeguarding approaches

Control access to sites	47%
Age restriction/filtering	41%
We can see what the children look at	62%
Children are only allowed online for a certain amount of time	48%
Children are not allowed online after a certain time	35%
Children are only allowed to go online in family rooms	40%
Monitoring apps on mobile devices	17%
Tracking apps on mobile devices	6%

a very broad and complex mix of issues that cause upset to them online. While this should, in an evidence-based policy forming approach, underpin any considerations of online safeguarding, as we will explore in Chapter 3, this is not necessarily borne out. Instead, we see a drive for solutions to a far narrower range of safeguarding issues that have potential political capital and media interest.

Notes

1 www.swgfl.org.uk/
2 www.surveymonkey.co.uk/r/ypinternet
3 Year groups are taken from the England/Wales school system, so year 4 pupils will be aged between 8 and 9, year 5 will be 9 and 10, year 6 will be 11 and 12, and so on.
4 Phippen (2018). "What Causes Upset Online?". https://swgfl.org.uk/assets/documents/what-causes-upset-online.pdf
5 The KSx notation next to each quotation refers to the "Key Stage" within which the respondent currently resides. Key Stages are groupings of years in the English education system – Key Stage 2 (KS2) comprises years 3 to 6, Key Stage 3 (KS3) is years 7 to 9 and Key Stage 4 (KS4) is years 10 to 11. www.gov.uk/national-curriculum
6 Phippen, A. and Phippen, H. (2018). "The UK government internet safety strategy – Time to listen to the youth voice?". *Entertainment Law Review*, 29(8).
7 Mumsnet (2018). "Survey Uncovers Parents' Top Online Safety Concerns". www.mumsnet.com/child/top-online-safety-concerns-for-parents?utm_source=Twitter&utm_medium=Tweet&utm_campaign=page+survey+iwf
8 Netsafe New Zealand (2018). "Parenting and Pornography: Findings from Australia, New Zealand and the United Kingdom". www.netsafe.org.nz/wp-content/uploads/2018/12/summary-report-parenting-and-pornography.pdf
9 OFCOM (2018). "Children and Parents: Media Use and Attitudes Report 2018". www.ofcom.org.uk/__data/assets/pdf_file/0024/134907/Children-and-Parents-Media-Use-and-Attitudes-2018.pdf

3 Safeguarding children by prohibiting access

Now that we have established what young people have told us that they consider upsetting in Chapter 2, we begin to explore the policy space and where technology is viewed as providing the solution to these issues. In this chapter we begin to look at how algorithms are used around safeguarding for children and the underpinning legislation and policy for this. As already introduced, the initial driver for this definition of online safety emerged from the All-Party Inquiry into Child Online Safety in 2012[1], and the Government cemented its commitment to this policy direction in 2013 and 2014 with the UK Prime Minister David Cameron making speeches about online child safety, one at the NSPCC[2] that we have already discussed briefly and one at WeProtect[3]. The focus of both speeches was on the need to protect children from what the speeches defined as the harmful content they might face online – namely access to adult pornography and also the production and distribution of Child Sexual Exploitation Material (CSEM). The resultant policy fall-out from these speeches was pressure applied to industry to *ensure* children cannot see harmful and sexual content and a growing expectation that filtering technology would be placed in the home to prevent young people from accessing "the Dark Side of the Web". Subsequent safeguarding statutory requirements by the UK Department for Education placed even great emphasis on the expectation of schools to ensure access to harmful content was controlled through monitoring the internet access of children. This chapter explores the technical interventions and shows both the pragmatic and effective, and then the less successful. It explores why some approaches work, and some do not, and also whether solutions, in actual fact, do much to safeguarding children and young people.

In the first speech by Mr Cameron, at the National Society for the Prevention of Cruelty to Children, in July 2013, he focussed on what he described at the two major child protection challenges:

> The fact is that the growth of the internet as an unregulated space has thrown up two major challenges when it comes to protecting our children.
>
> The first challenge is criminal: and that is the proliferation and accessibility of child abuse images on the internet.

The second challenge is cultural: the fact that many children are viewing online pornography and other damaging material at a very young age and that the nature of that pornography is so extreme, it is distorting their view of sex and relationships.

While we might disagree that these are the *only* two major child protection challenges in the online world, the focus of this early policy discussion has been very much around access to this *inappropriate* content.

There is some inconsistency in the speech given on the one hand it tries to differentiate between these two harms but also expects a single approach to tackling them:

Now, let me be clear, the two challenges are very distinct and very different. In one we're talking about illegal material, the other is legal material that is being viewed by those who are underage. But both the challenges have something in common; they're about how our collective lack of action on the internet has led to harmful and, in some cases, truly dreadful consequences for children.

Initially, Mr Cameron distinguished between the illegal aspect of CSEM, and the legal but age inappropriate nature of pornography[4], but he also said that a lack of action "on the Internet" results in the same impacts on children and young people. Within the policy area these generalisation scapegoating *the Internet*, or *online technology* are both rife and unhelpful. The implication in the speech is that similar routes to tackling these problems are needed, and those routes are technical in nature.

Yet we would argue that the two are very different indeed. In one case (CSEM), the child is the subject of abuse and exploitation and, in general, the issue is preventing adult access to CSEM images and videos. While there are some concerns around young people accessing CSEM, particularly around peer images[5], the majority of this material is produced, shared, and downloaded by adults. The other issue is trying to prevent young people from accessing pornography. The child in this case is not the subject of abuse, but the agent wishing to download the content (or, stumbling across it by accident). Prevention for these two scenarios seems to us to be very different tasks, which is why it is concerning that they are linked together in the original speech. We can see, very clearly, that such speeches have a policy impact, and drive industry change. Sometimes this is a good thing, and sometimes it is not. We can see, when we return to the online harms white paper in Chapter 4, that this policy direction eventually moved from an invitation to self-regulate to the imposition of legislation. However, in the early roots of this policy, there were clear successes in pressuring industry to change.

A number of successes were drawn from this policy pressure on industry, and showed engagement from the tech industry in dealing with access to CSEM.

Firstly, in terms of searching for CSEM and similar, the major search engine providers moved to block a number of search terms, and implement warnings on their search screens[6] if people searched for those terms. According to reporting, up to 100,000 search terms that have been used to categorise and index CSEM are included, and if an end user searches for these terms they will not yield any search results and will be presented with a warning (or "splash") screen about the legality of CSEM materials.

This list of terms is not made public, having been "drawn up by child protection experts". This would seem, on the one hand, sensible. If people were aware of what terms were being blocked, they would start classifying their content using other terms. However, one issue we will return to frequently in this text is the lack of transparency in the algorithms purporting to safeguard children online and, therefore, a lack of scrutiny regarding whether claimed functionalities are valid. If there is no way of knowing what these keywords are, or who has ownership over them, it is difficult to monitor feature creep or even authenticate the validity of the search terms.

Furthermore, the search engines were making use of the Internet Watch Foundation's URL and hash lists. The Internet Watch Foundation is a member organisation in the UK, funded by the technology sector, that has legislative powers to determine whether a web address (or Uniform Resource Locator – URL) provides access to CSEM. This determination is achieved either reactively as a result of a public report, or proactively (since 2014 when the UK government granted them additional legal powers[7]) searching websites to determine whether they contain it. If the organisation decides that the material the website provides meets the threshold to be considered CSEM under UK law (specifically the Protection of Children Act 1978[8]) the URL will be added to the IWF list. Then technology providers who either provide Internet access, or services that might allow access to websites (for example, search engines), can make use of the URL list to block access to these sites. The list is used extensively by service providers in the UK.

The other main service the IWF provide is a hash list. If images have been identified as CSEM, the image will be processed using Microsoft's PhotoDNA algorithms[9], a hashing technique as described in Chapter 1. Once the image has been identified and hashed using the Microsoft service, the hash will be stored in the IWF list. If a service provides access to images, it can then run the same PhotoDNA algorithm on any images it indexes, and if the hash matches, the platform knows, because it is in the IWF hash list, that the image has already been identified as CSEM and therefore illegal. PhotoDNA differs somewhat from more traditional hashing algorithms because, Microsoft claim, an image can be altered in some ways and the hash value will remain the same. One of the traditional problems with image hashes has been because it was applied on the data in the image (i.e. the image pixels, colour values, image size, etc.) the slightest change to the data (for example, resizing recolouring or cropping the image), the hash value would be different and therefore a match would not be made.

PhotoDNA will still produce the same hash, even if the image is changed "a little" and is therefore more robust than most hashing approaches.

The impact of this change in approach was reported to be significant. Mr Cameron, at WeProtect in December 2014, delivered an "update" on the previous speech:

> This landmark agreement we're signing amounts to nothing less than a global war against online child abuse. And this is a war we can only win if we fight it together. And we're fighting on three main fronts. First, blocking search results that lead to child abuse. Second, identifying the illegal images and taking them down. And third chasing down the perpetrators and enforcing the law … .
>
> … Until recently, it was incredibly easy for people to search the internet for child abuse and get results. And even sometimes have their search terms automatically completed for them. It was appalling. And yet, when we talked about changing it, a lot of people said, 'Can't be done. You can't police the internet. You can't infringe internet freedoms in any way.' But we said you can't have the freedom to search for vile material trumping a child's freedom to have an innocent childhood. So I made very clear the industry would have to find a way to block these search results and if they didn't then we would look at legislation.

A UK Government update on Tackling Child Sexual Exploitation[10] showed further progress, stating that Google has reported an eight-fold decrease in searches of CSEM on its search platform since the introduction of keyword blocks. Clearly, as a part of a larger approach to tackling illegal CSEM content online, these technical interventions were effective. If we are to reflect upon why this would be the case, there are a number of factors in its success.

The IWF makes it very clear on their website that any URL in their list has already been through a judgement against transparent legislation:

> The URLs are assessed according to UK law, specifically the Protection of Children Act 1978, and in accordance with the UK Sentencing Guidelines Council. All URLs added to the list depict indecent images of children, advertisements for or links to such content. This content is likely to be an offence to download, distribute, or possess in the UK. This includes pay-to-view websites as well as sites where child sexual abuse images are swapped, traded or posted.

And similarly, their hashing service has a level of transparency, and can therefore be subject to some scrutiny:[11]

> We turn child sexual abuse images into unique codes (hashes) – think of it as a digital fingerprint. We do this using Microsoft PhotoDNA. With our list, you'll be able to automatically match known images before they appear on your services. You'll also be able to remove illegal images already on your services. You'll receive an updated list every day.

The approach had a very clear technical and legal requirement – to tackle illegal CSEM material online. The boundaries of the requirements are defined in law, and as such eliminated ambiguity in the system. There was no need for an algorithm to make a subjective judgement on whether a piece of content was illegal. It had already been classified as such by a human analyst and hashed, another clearly defined and unambiguous operation for an algorithm to perform, such that if an image was attempted to be uploaded into any of the service provider's platforms again, it would easily be matched and prevented from being uploaded. Furthermore, by using the IWF URL list, it is a relatively simple (in technical terms) operation to prevent any website on that list appearing in search results.

In all of these elements, there are some key features:

- Clearly defined boundaries defined in legislation and with human analyst intervention (illegal content)
- Unambiguous and effective data processing (does one URL or hash match another?)
- Unambiguous and effective keyword or hash matching

This approach is successful because IT can work independently and objectively without any need for subjective judgement or outlying interpretation.

However, even within this success we must acknowledge this is not a complete solution. This will only prevent access to CSEM via search engines and, as reported upon by the IWF itself, the volume of child abuse images accessed via search engines[12] is not large compared to other sources such as image lockers or direct website access. However, there are clear successes to this strategy and we can see a technical solution that worked in certain scenarios.

If we now move on to another policy objective from these speeches, and one that has perhaps had a more problematic evolution, we can explore attempts to prevent children from accessing "legal" pornography.

UK schools have long adopted filtering approaches to ensure students in their establishments were not going to access pornography and other "inappropriate" materials, with varying levels of success[13]. Further statutory guidance was established in 2016 with the introduction of online safety to the Keeping Children Safe in Education guidance, which is now well established[14], that ensured all schools were legally responsible for filtering their Internet access. Within the main body of the report, specific mention of filtering and monitoring systems places the responsibility on the school board to ensure these technologies are in place.

> As schools and colleges increasingly work online, it is essential that children are safeguarded from potentially harmful and inappropriate online material. As such, governing bodies and proprietors should ensure appropriate filters and appropriate monitoring systems are in place.

Over-blocking is specifically mentioned within the guidance and, once again, the board is responsible to "ensure" that it does not take place:

> Whilst it is essential that governing bodies and proprietors ensure that appropriate filters and monitoring systems are in place, they should be careful that 'over blocking' does not lead to unreasonable restrictions as to what children can be taught with regard to online teaching and safeguarding.

Furthermore, in Appendix A of the same document, more detail is placed around what the filtering expectations are.

> Governing bodies and proprietors should be doing all that they reasonably can to limit children's exposure to the above risks from the school's or college's IT system. As part of this process, governing bodies and proprietors should ensure their school or college has appropriate filters and monitoring systems in place. Whilst considering their responsibility to safeguard and promote the welfare of children, and provide them with a safe environment in which to learn, governing bodies and proprietors should consider the age range of their pupils, the number of pupils, how often they access the IT system and the proportionality of costs vs risks. The appropriateness of any filters and monitoring systems are a matter for individual schools and colleges and will be informed in part, by the risk assessment required by the Prevent Duty.

Again, the term *appropriate* is applied, and there is an expectation that filtering goes beyond pornographic content. With the introduction of Prevent duties for schools in 2015[15], which aimed to tackle radicalisation, it was clear that terrorist material also needed to be blocked. While the guidance itself does not attempt to define what "appropriate" is, it does refer to the UK Safer Internet Centre's guidance[16] to schools on what appropriate filtering might comprise:

Blocking illegal content:
- Using IWF lists
- Integrate the 'the police assessed list of unlawful terrorist content, produced on behalf of the Home Office'

Blocking inappropriate online content:
- Discrimination
- Drugs/Substance abuse
- Extremism
- Malware/Hacking
- Pornography
- Piracy and copyright theft
- Self harm
- Violence

The advice states:

> This list should not be considered an exhaustive list and providers will be able to demonstrate how their system manages this content and many other aspects
>
> Providers should be clear how their system does not over block access so it does not lead to unreasonable restrictions.

Therefore once more placing the expectation on the providers (in this case filtering providers)to ensure all manner of content is blocked, but done so in a way where ambiguity is removed and over blocking does not take place. While this might be very easy to say in a definition of expectation, it is far more difficult to achieve in code. A number of the content types directed as *inappropriate* in a school setting have no definition in law, or even agreement in safeguarding. For example, if we are to expect to block all content related to "violence", they may be a significant challenge in controlling access to news articles that might report on violent acts. One example of this was the Manchester Arena bombing in 2017[17], which was reported as upsetting nine times in our survey on young people discussed in Chapter 2. Unsurprisingly all of these disclosures were taken in the months following the attack. Are we therefore suggesting that, given that the news can sometimes produce content that relates to violence, or extremism or radicalisation, and we have seen in Chapter 2 that young people report that "news" is the most likely term they will use to describe something they have seen that is upsetting, we should restrict young people's access to this in order to keep them safe? After all, this is content reporting on violence, and in some cases quite shocking. For example, the BBC News reporting of the murder of Lee Rigby was the subject of many complaints because of its graphic nature[18]. Furthermore, if we were to decide that algorithms had to block news content covering violent events, how might that actually be achieved in order that code might do this effectively? In the case of the coverage of the Lee Rigby murder, some of the upsetting content was live streamed on BBC news platforms. An algorithm would have no way of determining the upset within a live stream, that would have to be managed to human intervention and editorial policy (something mentioned in the OFCOM bulletin on the BBC news reporting in this case).

The term *inappropriate* is frequently used in the child safeguarding space to describe types of content deemed unsuitable for children to view. A dictionary definition[19] of "inappropriate" is useful if we are to consider algorithmic approaches to controlling access to content:

> Not suitable or proper in the circumstances.

The concept of inappropriate, which might potentially be something that is achievable through human intervention, is far more challenging for an algorithm. While we, as humans, might be able to make a sound, albeit subjective, judgement when viewing a piece of content whether or not it would be appropriate for a young person to see it, this comprises a level of subjective judgement very difficult to establish in code. It is based upon experience, the capability to actually view and interpret the content, the capacity to apply one's own subjective morality (related to the cultural norm) to the piece of content, and a level of emotional intelligence that would understand what might upset a young person and why. None of this is particularly achievable in code – which relies upon precise rules, or training data (see Chapter 5) if it is to attempt to be interpretive. Without these facets, we would have to fall back upon what has already been discussed – blocking based upon keywords and URL lists. However in this case, without clear legal definition, we would rely upon a specific individual, or individual's moral intepretation to make the judgement of what is inappropriate. Even when dealing with clearly illegal content, such as that addressed by the IWF, there still needs to be a human interpretation of the content in order to blacklist or take down a URL. If we were to expand this model of blocking/intervention to a level to tackle inappropriate content, the overheads might become massive.

One attempt to tackle one form of inappropriate content – that related to extremism and radicalisation – is well established in UK blocking and filtering scenarios, but highlights the complexities of blocking inappropriate, rather than illegal, content. The Counter Terrorism Internet Referral Unit[20], provides a list of URLs, similar to the IWF list, that are judged to be serving up terrorist content. It has been reported[21] that the organisation has listed over 150,000 separate URLs, provided by the unit itself and law enforcement partners. While this might be considered good practice, given the maintenance of a list that is readily available to service providers, there are concerns[22]. The main concern relates to excessive and opaque filtering of online content that, given the lack of scrutiny on the list, or any transparency to the unit's operation, has become a list maintained in secret. Therefore, there has to be a level of subjectivity to the list, which, as we have already discussed, presents problems for algorithms. But it also presents challenges on a more moral level, as we have no way of scrutinising this list. It also means that those whose sites might end up on such a list, perhaps inappropriately, have no recourse to address this, or even an awareness that they have been blocked. The IWF list is clearly established against a legislation that clearly defines content served as illegal based upon well-established, and tested, legislation. There is no such legislation that clearly defines how a piece of content might be judged to be terrorist. Once a URL has been judged to be illegal, the IWF has powers to launch legal proceedings against the site (if it is in UK jurisdiction) or pass to law enforcement partners who can act. This is not the case with a list that is managed against content that cannot be judged as illegal. Therein lies one of the fundamental challenges of tackling inappropriate or harmful, but not illegal, content.

While schools have been subject to requirements for Internet filtering for a number of years, the UK government was keen, in its mission to "protect children from the darkest corners of the Internet" to move this functionality into the home as well. Unsurprisingly perhaps, given previous discussions in this text, the expectation for this provision lay at the hands of the internet service providers.

By the end of 2013, the Government had forged an agreement with the largest four ISPs in the UK, under which the ISPs committed to offering all new customers a network level filtering service, in the face of a threat to ISPs that if they didn't do something voluntarily, the Government would legislate.

The focus of responsibly lay with industry, and the threat of legislation loomed if they were not to do what they were asked. And clearly the Westminster perspective was that this approach has worked because on both occasions industry did respond and provide "solutions" – once the ISPs providing home filtering and once search engine providers restricted access to child abuse images in their search results. However, the actual success of the approaches to stop young people accessing pornography is debatable and poorly evidenced.

Within this first wave of pornography prevention *solutions* we also saw the introduction of "Family Friendly WiFi"[23] – in order that public WiFi access in the UK was filtered to prevent access to CSEM and pornography (and other "inappropriate" content):

> Simply tell us what type of websites you want to block – Adult Content, Illegal Content, Streaming Media, Chat & Instant Messaging, Social Networking, etc. – and we'll do the rest. Our proprietary internet filtering algorithms intelligently categorize sites so you don't have to constantly maintain a list of blocked sites.

Again, the differentiation of the legal and illegal is a complex one to marry into the same service, and we might reflect, probably should not be offered in one solution. Running the IWF URL list means that illegal content related to CSEM can be effectively managed and it is unlikely that even the most freedom-craving Internet libertarian would argue that this material should be accessible in a café WiFi hotspot. However, other forms of content blocking become more problematic and face similar problems of over-blocking than a lot of other filtering services which we will address in more detail later.

While the introduction of Family Friend WiFi, and the resultant impact of this on other providers (i.e. they also began to filter on public WiFi)[24] was viewed as a child protection success, perhaps with some reflection this might not be as significant a technical achievement as it was hailed. As this section is being written the author is sat in a well-known coffee chain using their public "family friendly" WiFi. There are, as I might expect, blocks to sites such as Pornhub and XVideos. However, it also prevented access to a number of websites related to sexuality (www.iusw.org, www.seriouslysexuality.com), LGBT community sites (barnet-gay.co.uk, www.guide-gay.com), the inexplicable (www.christiansagainstpoverty.org, www.swordforum.com/), and perhaps the most unfortunately named online business – Pen Island Pens (www.penisland.net/). It also failed to prevent to access pornography via Twitter and Reddit.

Admittedly, filters continue to improve, as more URLs become "white listed" – where innocuous websites were previously blocked, by reporting the block filtering providers will add them to a list which will mean that even if the filtering algorithm detects a reason to block (for example, sexual keywords in the URL or website content), the white list will override this decision and allow the site access. This, of itself, seems a curious process. A business, NGO, or individual establishing a website to provide some form of service which then, due to the filtering algorithms, ends up being blocked on either public WIFI provision or home filtering (both use similar technology and in a number of cases share the same lists), so the provider then needs to make a report to each filtering company to ask for their (entirely legal and in no way contentious) web content to be whitelisted. In essence, they need to contact the filtering providers and say "please can you not block my website, I promise it's not pornographic or harmful to children", a highly curious process in a liberal democracy that claims to value freedom of expression.

Moreover, there is a more fundamental issue, and that is does filtering public WiFi actually solve a real problem? While it is unquestionable that any internet service provision should prevent access to illegal content, and this is why the IWF services are so well regarded and successful, is the goal of preventing children accessing pornography in cafes, libraries, and supermarkets a problem we needed to tackle? There is a twofold "protection" measure here – first to prevent children from accessing pornography, and second to prevent children seeing an adult accessing pornography. We have posed this question at many conferences with both fellow academics and many professionals in the children's workforce, we always seem to come to the same conclusion – this is not something we see. While it would be difficult to argue that children and young people, or even adults, *should* be allowed to access pornography in public space, we would suggest that both should be entitled to access sites related to sex education, gender and human rights, mental health services, or any number of other innocuous sites on an internet connection. Yet family-friendly WiFi remains something that is viewed as a step forward in algorithmic child safeguarding, even if the problem it is tackling has little evidence of existing.

Returning to the more general issue around the introduction of filters in the home in 2013, all major Internet Service Providers now provide a suite of filtering solutions to the home to ensure that children could not access pornography on home devices. After considerable government pressure, new subscribers had a default "opt in" to these services – when they establish a new connection the filters are switched on, and the subscriber has to make an active choice to switch them off. Existing subscribers were given the choice to install filters. This voluntary response to policy pressure was put in place in 2013, so has now be available to subscribers for over five years. We have seen from the discussion in Chapter 2 that from our parent's survey with MumsNet, as well as data from young people we surveyed, that around 40% of parents chose to have filters switched on. OFCOM's recently published Media Literacy report 2018[25] reports a figure of 34% of parents of 5–15-year-olds installing filters. After five years of media reporting, service provider and government nudge and policy drive, filters are still not used in half of the homes in the UK. The same report stated that over blocking was rarely a reason for parents not to install filters (the most popular reason being they preferred to establish their own "rules" in the home for addressing internet access). Which does raise the question – if these technologies are effective, why wouldn't parents install them in the home?

We have, in this chapter, explored two aspects of filtering that have been viewed as policy successes in the UK, the blocking of illegal content, and the establishment of more widespread filtering of legal content that is considered inappropriate for children in both public spaces and in the home. We have also seen different levels of success with these approaches, particularly when reflecting upon the effectiveness of the technology, and the potential overreliance on it (the central argument of this text). While we have shown why a narrow filter against clearly defined illegal content is successful, we cannot report such successes with the broader use of filters. At the time of writing, the Blocked project, run by the Open Rights Group[26], which scans URLs against ISP filters to determine levels of overblocking, had submitted over 40 million URLs to internet filters and identified 759,673 blocks, 21,745 of which are suspect false positives. This would suggest around 3% of URLs blocked by these filters are done so incorrectly. Which does illustrate why filtering cannot be as effective as some would like. The Open Rights Group, alongside Top10VPN reported on this in 2019[27]. The report states quite correctly:

> There is no evidence that filters are preventing children from seeing adult content or keeping them safe online. They may be contributing to a lack of resilience that can increase risk to children.

The main reason for such problems lies within the problem domain itself – the requirements placed on filtering are poorly and ambiguously defined, and feature creep is rife. While the original policy direction was almost entirely focussed on pornography, we have seen that there is now an expectation on filters to control access to all manner of other content, such as self-harm, terrorism, violence, drugs and alcohol, gambling, and discrimination. None of which are easy to define in law, let alone code, and therefore somewhat problematic for an algorithm to address.

If we remain focussed on pornography for now, we can, as humans, make a fairly good judgement on whether a piece of content is pornographic. However, history has shown that obscenity, and pornography, have troubled law makers. Rather famously, in 1963, in the US case of *Jacobellis v Ohio*[28], where the Supreme Court was ruling on whether a movie (Louis Malle's *The Lovers*) was obscene, the Supreme Court Justice Potter Stewart, confirming our observation above about the role subjective interpretation plays in deciding whether something is pornographic, was quoted as saying

> I shall not today attempt further to define the kinds of material I understand to be embraced within that shorthand description ["hard-core pornography"], and perhaps I could never succeed in intelligibly doing so. But I know it when I see it, and the motion picture involved in this case is not that.[29]

He made this statement in an attempt to explain why the material was not considered obscene under the Roth Test[30]. The Roth Test itself defines material to be obscene if:

> to the average person, applying contemporary community standards, the dominant theme of the material, taken as a whole, appeals to prurient interest.

In more modern times, the legislation still struggles to define something in a clear, objective (and therefore algorithmically possible) manner. In the legislation we will be exploring in more detail later in this chapter, the 2017 Digital Economy Act[31] finally produced a legal definition for pornography:

> In this Part 'pornographic material' (except in the expression 'extreme pornographic material') means any of the following—
>
> (a) a video work in respect of which the video works authority has issued an R18 certificate;
> (b) material that was included in a video work to which paragraph (a) applies, if it is reasonable to assume from its nature that its inclusion was among the reasons why the certificate was an R18 certificate;
> (c) any other material if it is reasonable to assume from its nature that any classification certificate issued in respect of a video work including it would be an R18 certificate;
> (d) a video work in respect of which the video works authority has issued an 18 certificate, and that it is reasonable to assume from its nature was produced solely or principally for the purposes of sexual arousal;
> (e) material that was included in a video work to which paragraph (d) applies, if it is reasonable to assume from the nature of the material—
>   (i) that it was produced solely or principally for the purposes of sexual arousal, and
>   (ii) that its inclusion was among the reasons why the certificate was an 18 certificate;
> (f) any other material if it is reasonable to assume from its nature—
>   (i) that it was produced solely or principally for the purposes of sexual arousal, and
>   (ii) that any classification certificate issued in respect of a video work including it would be an 18 certificate;
> (g) a video work that the video works authority has determined not to be suitable for a classification certificate to be issued in respect of it, if—
>   (i) it includes material (other than extreme pornographic material) that it is reasonable to assume from its nature was produced solely or principally for the purposes of sexual arousal, and
>   (ii) it is reasonable to assume from the nature of that material that its inclusion was among the reasons why the video works authority made that determination;

(h) material (other than extreme pornographic material) that was included in a video work that the video works authority has determined not to be suitable for a classification certificate to be issued in respect of it, if it is reasonable to assume from the nature of the material—

   (i) that it was produced solely or principally for the purposes of sexual arousal, and

   (ii) that its inclusion was among the reasons why the video works authority made that determination;

(i) any other material (other than extreme pornographic material) if it is reasonable to assume from the nature of the material—

   (i) that it was produced solely or principally for the purposes of sexual arousal, and

   (ii) that the video works authority would determine that a video work including it was not suitable for a classification certificate to be issued in respect of it.

In this rather detailed definition, there are three key factors at play:

- The content would be classified at R18
- The content would be classified as 18, and was solely produced for the purposes of sexual arousal
- The content was solely produced for the purposes of sexual arousal

If we first consider whether a piece of content would be classified with the BBFC ratings[32] of either R18 or 18, we should understand how this is judged. The BBFC would, generally, give a classification based upon a human moderator viewing a piece of content and making a judgement upon it. The second point regarding sexual arousal is also a somewhat ambiguous one. While the physiology and psychology of sexual arousal fall outside of the scope of this text, we might agree that there is a level of subjectivity there – one person's arousing content might not be the same as another. It is for this reason that, in general, obscenity is something that will be debated in the courts, and even then, as we have already highlighted with the famous *Jacobellis v Ohio* case, there is a high degree of subjectivity.

Yet the policy direction seems to be expecting technology providers to start to automate this process. How, given the subjectivity of the interpretation of the definition in the Digital Economy Act legislation, and the need for subjective interpretation and debate, around whether a piece of content is sexually arousing, can we possibly expect this to be implemented in code? While Chapter 5 will explore in far greater detail how *artificial intelligence* is increasingly being applied as a proposed "solution" to this ambiguity but, as we will see in that discussion, we are still reliant on data processing and training data as a means to make subjective interpretations. Moreover, these are not, in the human sense, subjective interpretations. The algorithms are not interpreting in the slightest, they are making evaluations based upon past data within a set statistical threshold to make a judgement on whether the piece of content or webpage is similar in data composition to others it has been shown. Algorithms are extremely poor at subjectivity – they need things defined as rules that are clear and precise. If we, as humans, cannot agree on whether a piece of content is sexually arousing, how can we expect a piece of code to do so? Which is why filters still have to rely on keywords matching and URL lists. And why they are imperfect as a solution.

And while some might argue that a little over-blocking is an acceptable outcome for ensuring that children and young people cannot see harmful content, we should make two points. Firstly, as we have shown previously, even on a strong public filter, it is very easy to access content that should definitely have been blocked given the filtering policy. And secondly, is it a price worth paying to prevent access to useful, educative content while trying to control access to other more harmful materials?

A key tenant of the Digital Economy Act is that pornography providers implement age verification technology to ensure anyone using their services in the UK is over the age of 18. Again, this highlights the ideological position that technology has to be the solution to these issues. And again, we might suggest that those who have defined the policy are not particularly well versed in the ways of code and online technologies.

While a lot of the discussion around the age verification legislation is beyond the scope of this text. Our focus is on what technology can, and cannot, do related to online safeguarding and child protection. However, it is worthwhile to explore this as the, at the time of writing, endpoint conclusions to the UK government's commitment to ensuring children and young people cannot see pornography. Evidence that government views this as the endpoint comes from scant reference to pornography in the Online Harms white paper, and what there is centres upon the fact that the forthcoming age verification solution(s) will address this.

If we are to consider the requirements for age verification, a fundamental issue facing any solution in the UK is that there is no established ID or age verification system in the UK that encompasses the population as a whole. While we can argue things such as passports, drivers licence, credit cards, or mobile phone contracts have some application to the age verification problem space, their purpose is for something other than that, and ownership is certainly not a statutory requirement. Therefore, we are placing an expectation on the adult population, if they wish to access entirely legal content, they have to divulge some form of token-based age verification. With the dearth of blanket age verification solution, we might be placing an expectation upon adults to enrol in a system for which they do not wish to engage, in order to access perfectly legal online content.

The Government's consultation around Age Verification[33] raised the "success" of the German system established by the *Kommission für Jugendmedienschutz* (KfJ) in 2003[34]. At its inception, this system required some level of "opt in" through either a mobile phone-based authentication or registration at a local post office. The Deutsche Post AG service required attendance at a local post office to obtain age verification which is entered into a central database. However, that authentication is based upon the legally required ID card, something that is not in place in the UK. A mobile phone–based authentication via Vodafone D2 using the phone's SIM is used, so again places a token-based requirement on the subscriber even if they have no wish to own one. While more age verification modules have been added to the system as it matured, a final point on the KfJ approach is that the age verification on adult content only exists for pornography providers hosted in Germany – those whose domains are restricted to .de addresses. The system is limited in geography, something that the UK government's proposals are not.

Part of the logic applied to this debate was that age verification already exists in offline settings (for example, the sale of cigarettes and alcohol, cinemas, solvent purchases, etc.). It has also raised the argument that other online services already have a level of age verification, for example, gambling, some gaming apps and services, and similar. However, with a face-to-face purchase, we have in place multiple age verification factors such as financial authentication and a visual judgement of the buyer by the seller. For online issues such as gambling, one of the fundamental requirements to engage with services is you have to have a financial capability to do so. Which means being in possession of a credit card or online payment system, which would imply an adult. There is, for some services, no financial requirement to engage with pornography – one does not need to have to buy the content, revenue is generated from advertising income. Therefore, the age-verification requirement is less financially driven and token-based approaches are less likely to succeed.

Moreover, in the online world we have seen for years a classic age verification issue that has never been resolved – under 13s on social media. While the providers make it clear this is unacceptable and they are mindful to respond to legislative demands, their response is reactive. While platform providers will respond to a report of an underaged user and remove them, others in society who do not wish to follow this rule (for example, parents or the young users themselves) are not technologically prohibited and there are frequent pieces of research showing the volume of underaged users on those sites[35]. The key issues with this age verification is that there is no specific token-based means for age verification at the age of 13 (how does one "prove" they are 13?), therefore there is little the provider can to do check, outside of asking for a date of birth and agreement with terms and conditions where the user agrees that they are above the age required for the site. Within the emergent Online Harms White Paper there seems to be further pressure to return to this issue. Which is somewhat confusing given that the 13 age limit was never one that related to safeguarding, harm or even child development. It was, instead, concerned with advertising legislation in the first instance (the Children's Online Piracy Protection Act[36] in the US) and subsequently data protection legislation. More recently, in the case of the UK, the implementation of the General Data Protection Regulation[37] – the Data Protection Act 2018 – places a requirement in line with the age of 13 for the capability of a young person to consent to their data being processed for any online service[38]. While there are clear legislative reasons for the need for age verifications, these do not relate to online harms. They instead are concerned that a child has to have the capacity to consent to their data being collected.

The Digital Economy Act makes it clear that any commercial pornography provider allowing access to their services from the UK must provide age verification to ensure only people over the age of 18 are allowed on. The term *commercial* does not necessarily relate to pay for access services. A site making income from advertising but providing pornography for free would be equally accountable. One of the interesting questions around this legislation is what actually constitutes a pornography provider – given there is much pornography on much more broad social platforms (for example, as discussed earlier in this chapter, Twitter and Reddit). A statutory instrument was published to clarify this – The Online Pornography (Commercial Basis) Regulations 2019[39]. In this instrument, it is stated that a site or application would not be subject to age verification if it comprises less than one-third of its content is pornographic. How one third of content is judged is not defined in the instrument, so we do not know whether this relates to file capacity (i.e. the amount of pornographic content in megabytes/total site content in megabytes), file count (i.e. given the number of files on the site, are over one third pornographic) or whether this relates to overall content (for example, administration and other publicly inaccessible files), or only files that could potentially be served to an end user.

Nevertheless, the British Board of Film Classification (BBFC)[40] was appointed as the Age Verification regulator, responsible for the enforcement section of the Digital Economy Act legislation. It was granted powers (that come into force of July 15 2019) to enforce the legislation including the means to request social media companies and search engines to remove services, request withdrawal of service from payment providers, and instructing Internet Service Providers to block non-compliant sites. They can also impose financial penalties on non-complaint sites and will also provide the means for the public to report non-compliant sites, should they wish.

The list of potential powers places enormous resource implications on the regulator – with over 1 billion websites in existence, with an estimated 4% of those being pornographic[41], that is a considerable volume to monitor. By targeting those within the supply chain instead, threats to "lose UK-based income streams" suggests an attempt to place pressure on those companies outside of UK jurisdiction, which also raises questions when trying to determine a model where fining non-UK based companies might work. A number of these measures imply wide-ranging censoring powers for a regulator that would be operating outside of its geographic boundaries. It is therefore interesting to note that as the regulator, the BBFC was granted contingent liability from the UK government[42] in order that:

> The contingent liability will provide indemnity to the British Board of Film Classification (BBFC) against legal proceedings brought against the BBFC in its role as the age verification regulator for online pornography.

This is an interesting reflection which shows some concern on the part of the government, and regulator, that the application of legislative powers might result in legal challenges that the regulator was not comfortable accepting liability for.

It should be reiterated that both legislator and regulator state that the implementation of age verification by pornography providers is not their concern, and they expected to see many different options. Therefore, the choice of technology lies with the providers themselves, while the age verification scenario is essentially the same:

1. An end user in the UK wishes to access a pornography provider
2. The pornography provider detects that the end user is using a UK based IP address and triggers the age verification process
3. The end user verifies their age in some way (see next)
4. The end user is provided with some form of authentication to access the service once age is verified
5. The end user accesses the pornographic website

Choice of age verification technology is not yet in place, and apparently will not be until the law is enacted in July 2019. However, a number of technical approaches are proposed:

- Tok-based verification with something like a driving licence, passport, credit card, or mobile phone interaction in a fairly typical signup service but providers say personal data will not be stored once verification takes place
- Blockchain technology that will use similar token-based authentication but stored in different way to guarantee
- Facial recognition that uses "age estimation" technology to determine whether the end user
- Voucher or card-based authentication, which requires the purchase of a card from, for example, a newsagent, which holds a unique string that has to be validated by the app within a set number of hours after purchase

While there are lots of variations on a theme, all follow a fairly basic authentication based upon some token, followed by access. However, there are a number of concerns with both the effectiveness of the systems, and also privacy concerns that might arise.

There are serious concerns around privacy – of course, someone's pornography browsing habits might be considered valuable commercial data, given the potential market intelligence that might be gleaned, as well as the sensitive nature of someone's sexual interests and browsing history. Certainly, civil rights organisations such as the Open Rights Group have raised concerns[43], with some validity given previous leaks such as Ashley Maddison[44]. In this breach 25 gigabytes of data were shared online about people who had signed up to the service, which claimed to introduce users to "people who want to cheat". The release of real names, addresses, credit card numbers, and search histories were obviously severely distressing to those who might have been named, and there were some suggested links to suicides as a result of abuse received.

One can imagine similar levels of impact should a large database of end user's pornography habits and search histories being leaked. While the BBFC have developed a voluntary privacy scheme, the Age-verification Certification[45], there is no expectation that all age verification providers will have to adopt the scheme. Moreover, the certification was developed without public consultation or scrutiny, which places concerns around efficacy. We should be mindful that data related to one's sex life and sexual orientation is defined as "sensitive personal data" under the GDPR and Data Protection Act. One might reasonably suggest that an individual's pornography preferences should very much fall into this category, given it would expose the individual's pornographic preferences. Which means that processing of this information should only be carried out under certain conditions with explicit consent from the data subject. The GDPR extends the requirement that any data processing needs to be undertaken based upon the six data processing principles defined in the regulation, by demanding that there is a requirement that the processing of sensitive data meets at least one of six data protection conditions:

- Consent of the data subject
- Necessary for the performance of a contract with the data subject or to take steps preparatory to such a contract
- Necessary for compliance with a legal obligation
- Necessary to protect the vital interests of a data subject or another person where the data subject is incapable of giving consent
- Necessary for the performance of a task carried out in the public interest or in the exercise of official authority vested in the controller
- Necessary for the purposes of legitimate interests

Perhaps this is one of the reasons to indemnify the BBFC against liability under the legislation?

It remains to be seen whether this is well considered under the BBFC's certification scheme or age verification solutions that might choose to not engage with any voluntary privacy arrangements. It will equally be interesting to see as case law develops whether courts consider any of the conditions for processing being met within this age verification scenario.

The voucher-based systems, which involve a face to face age verification, alongside the purchase of a unique identifier to facilitate access to adult services with complete anonymity are an interesting mix of technology with human intervention and would certainly circumvent privacy concerns under the GDPR. The anonymity afforded by the service might appeal to the privacy aware pornography user. It is certainly an interesting proposition. However, there are a couple of more ideological issues that might present problems with this solution. First, there is a payment for the vouchers, so we are expecting adults to pay for access to services they are legally entitled to use, and are, in any other jurisdiction, free. And from a youth safeguarding perspective, a slightly more esoteric concern – might we envisage a marketplace for the resale of these vouchers to those perhaps not old enough to obtain them legally in the store?

Perhaps a more fundamental facet to this debate is will it actually work? Will age-verification technology on pornography sites when accessed from a specific geographical location result in children and young people being able to access adult content? Undoubtedly, it will go some way to preventing young people from accidentally stumbling across pornography is *some* scenarios, and there is research that says their first experiences of pornography were as likely to be accidental as deliberate[46]. However, in our own experiences with young people[47], there are also many determined young people who will actively seek it out.

We have already raised the issue of access to pornography via social media platforms, and this will have little impact upon this. While the BBFC have powers to

> notify them [social media companies] and request that they take action against non-compliant pornographic services – for example by removing accounts on social media.

It would be unlikely that large, non-UK–based organisations would respond to a request from outside of their jurisdiction that might impact their business model.

We have also had many conversations with young people about both pornography filtering and age verification and most believe this will have little impact upon them, or their peers, accessing pornography. There are, firstly, a number of technical approaches that can be used to bypass the age-verification system and it would seem that those who proposed and implementing this legislation had very little understanding of the global nature of the technology that underpins online technology. We have seen similar measures used on digital content indexing services such as The Pirate Bay, and we have also seen many approaches to get around such localised blocking via proxying, mirroring, and virtual private networks. All of these techniques could work to bypass any location-based blocking of pornography providers who do not comply with the intended UK legislation. Put simply – if the provider's system isn't aware that the request is coming from the UK, the age-verification system will not be triggered. Plenty of technology exists to hide, mask, or spoof an end user's IP address. While approaches such as Virtual Private Networks tend to have some cost implication, this is not the case with a proxying service, which will intercept a connection to an online service and change the source IP address to something else. And while proxying services can sometimes become overloaded and slow, this is not the case with browsers such as TOR, which are both free and designed to obfuscate the end user's IP address and traceability.

We should also acknowledge that in order for age verification to work in the home, devices need to be logged out, and usernames and passwords not retained, when an adult who has exercised a legal right to access to pornography decides to end their browsing session. Might the old school scenario of a teenager discovering a stash of pornographic magazines in their parent's bedroom be replicated in a modern digital way with calls to "come over, my dad's left his porn logged in". The BBFC claim that:

> Some determined teenagers will find ways to access pornography.

We would suggest they are massively underestimating the determination of teen-agers to get around technical blocks. Plus, the availability of information to do this. Concerns regarding children's rights in this area are well-founded and the intangibility of the *do more* mantra levelled at industry is also viewed as problem-atic by UNICEF[48]:

> Current public policy is increasingly driven by overemphasized, albeit real, risks faced by children online, with little consideration for potential negative impacts on children's rights to freedom of expression and access to informa-tion. The ICT sector, meanwhile, is regularly called on to reduce these risks, yet given little direction on how to ensure that children remain able to par-ticipate fully and actively in the digital world.

However, there is also a troubling premise to the BBFC statement that age verifica-tion will work because "most teenagers aren't bright enough to get around it". It does not require *all* teenagers to be technically competent to the level where they can bypass age verification solutions. Sharing large quantities of digital media over portable devices is something that is very easy, and cheap, to do. Access in whatever manner a young person is capable of achieving need only take place once, before harvesting of massive amounts of content and sharing with peers. The full impact of this "world first" as a step to making the UK the "safest place to go online in the world" remains to be seen. However, a more fundamental issue is will this make children and young people *safe*, or will it simply prevent them from developing resilience and knowledge around a sensitive topic such that, when they turn 18 and all the potential for control ceases, they can browse to their heart's content. This is not a safety measure, it is kicking the can down the road.

In this chapter, we have explored an ideological obsession in control through filtering and blocking. We have also discussed how, at a technical level, it will not achieve its goals. However, this is not the only approach to online safeguarding. In Chapter 4, we explore further the technologies that have been proposed as safeguarding "solutions", focussing upon monitoring, its origins and how it is evolving, and how that impacts on children's rights.

Notes

1 Independent Parliamentary Inquiry into Online Child Protection (2012). "Findings and Recommendations". www.safermedia.org.uk/Images/final-report.pdf
2 UK Government (2013). "The Internet and Pornography: Prime Minister Calls For Action". www.gov.uk/government/speeches/the-internet-and-pornogra-phy-prime-minister-calls-for-action
3 UK Government (2014). "#WeProtect Children Online Global Summit: Prime Minister's Speech". www.gov.uk/government/speeches/weprotect-children-online-global-summit-prime-ministers-speech
4 While there are some that might refer to CSEM as "child pornography" this will not be the case in this text. The distinction between legal pornography and indecent images of children and child abuse needs to be clear. By referring to it as

"child pornography" we are both failing to acknowledge the severity of abuse in the images, and also linking it legal material accepted in society as both acceptable and sexually arousing.

5 Phippen, A., Bond, E., and Tyrrell, K. (2018). "Peer on Peer Abuse – A National Survey of Headteachers and Safeguarding Leads in England and Scotland". www.mariecollinsfoundation.org.uk/assets/news_entry_featured_image/MCF-Peer-on-peer-Abuse-Research-Report-sunday-final-version.pdf
6 BBC News (2013). "Google and Microsoft agree steps to block abuse images". www.bbc.co.uk/news/uk-24980765
7 Ross, T. (2013). "Internet Watch Foundation Given Powers to Police Child Porn".www.telegraph.co.uk/news/politics/10127862/Internet-Watch-Foundation-given-powers-to-police-child-porn.html
8 UK Government (1978). "Protection of Children Act 1978". www.legislation.gov.uk/ukpga/1978/37/body/1991-02-01?timeline=true
9 https://news.microsoft.com/2009/12/15/new-technology-fights-child-porn-by-tracking-its-photodna/#sm.0001mpmupctevct7pjn11vtwrw6xj
10 UK Government (2017). "Tackling Child Sexual Exploitation Progress Report". https://assets.publishing.service.gov.uk/government/uploads/system/uploads/attachment_data/file/592588/Tackling_Child_Sexual_Exploitation_-_Progress_Report__web_.pdf
11 Albeit within the limitation of transparency that the functionality of Microsoft's PhotoDNA algorithm is not in the public domain. However, it is freely available to approved agencies so there is a level of openness and portability.
12 Internet Watch Foundation (2015). "Emerging Patterns and Trends Report #1 Online-Produced Sexual Content". www.iwf.org.uk/sites/default/files/inline-files/Online-produced_sexual_content_report_100315.pdf
13 Hope, A. (2008). "Internet pollution discourses, exclusionary practices and the 'culture of over-blocking' within UK schools". *Technology, Pedagogy and Education*, 17(2).
14 UK Government (2018). "Keeping Children Safe in Education – Statutory Guidance For Schools and Colleges". https://assets.publishing.service.gov.uk/government/uploads/system/uploads/attachment_data/file/741314/Keeping_Children_Safe_in_Education__3_September_2018_14.09.18.pdf
15 UK Government (2015). "Protecting Children From Radicalisation: The Prevent Duty". www.gov.uk/government/publications/protecting-children-from-radicalisation-the-prevent-duty
16 UK Safer Internet Centre (n.d.). "Appropriate Filtering". www.saferinternet.org.uk/advice-centre/teachers-and-school-staff/appropriate-filtering-and-monitoring/appropriate-filtering
17 Wikipedia (n.d.). "Manchester Arena Bombing". https://en.wikipedia.org/wiki/Manchester_Arena_bombing
18 OFCOM (2014). "OFCOM Broadcast Bulletin 245". www.ofcom.org.uk/__data/assets/pdf_file/0024/42837/obb245.pdf
19 Oxford Dictionaries (n.d.). "Inappropriate". https://en.oxforddictionaries.com/definition/inappropriate
20 Wikipedia (n.d.). "Counter Terrorism Referral Unit". https://en.wikipedia.org/wiki/Counter-Terrorism_Internet_Referral_Unit
21 UK Parliament (2016). "Counter-terrorism: Written Question – 30893". www.parliament.uk/business/publications/written-questions-answers-statements/written-question/Commons/2016-03-14/30893/
22 Open Rights Group (2018). "UK Internet Regulation Part I: Internet Censorship in the UK Today". www.openrightsgroup.org/assets/files/pdfs/reports/Internet_Regulation_Part_I_Internet_Censorship_in_the_UK_today-web.pdf
23 Friendly Wifi (n.d.). "About Friendly Wifi". www.friendlywifi.com/about

24 UK Safer Internet Centre (2015). "1st Anniversary of the Digital Friendly WiFi Accreditation Scheme". www.saferinternet.org.uk/blog/1st-anniversary-digital-friendly-wifi-accreditation-scheme
25 OFCOM (2019). "Children and Parents Media Use and Attitudes: Annex 1". www.ofcom.org.uk/__data/assets/pdf_file/0027/134892/Children-and-Parents-Media-Use-and-Attitudes-Annex-1.pdf
26 www.blocked.org.uk/
27 Top 10 VPN (2019). "Collateral Damage in the War Against Online Harms How Charities, Schools, and Social Support Websites Are Blocked by UK ISP Adult Content Filters". www.top10vpn.com/assets/2019/04/Top10VPN-and-ORG-Report-Collateral-Damage-in-the-War-Against-Online-Harms.pdf
28 US Supreme Court (n.d.). "*Jacobellis v. Ohio*, 378 U.S. 184 (1964)". https://supreme.justia.com/cases/federal/us/378/184/
29 Lattman, P (2007). "The Origins of Justice Stewart's 'I Know It When I See It'". https://blogs.wsj.com/law/2007/09/27/the-origins-of-justice-stewarts-i-know-it-when-i-see-it/
30 US Supreme Court (n.d.). "*Roth v. United States*, 354 U.S. 476 (1957)". https://supreme.justia.com/cases/federal/us/354/476/
31 UK Government (2017). "Digital Economy Act 2017 – Part 3". www.legislation.gov.uk/ukpga/2017/30/part/3/enacted
32 BBFC (n.d.). "Ratings Info". www.bbfc.co.uk/what-classification/what-bbfc-ratings-info
33 UK Government (2016). "Government Commitment to Protect Children from Online Pornography". www.gov.uk/government/news/government-commitment-to-protect-children-from-online-pornography
34 Palzer, C. (2003). "IRIS 2003-10:14/30 Germany: Age Verification System Standards for Youth Protection". http://merlin.obs.coe.int/iris/2003/10/article30.en.html
35 BBC News (2016). "Safer Internet Day: Young ignore 'social media age limit'". www.bbc.co.uk/news/education-35524429
36 FTC (1998). "Children's Online Privacy Protection Rule ("COPPA")". www.ftc.gov/enforcement/rules/rulemaking-regulatory-reform-proceedings/childrens-online-privacy-protection-rule
37 European Union (2016). "General Data Protection Regulation". https://gdpr-info.eu
38 UK Government (2018). "Data Protection Act 2018 – Part 2, Chapter 2, Section 9". www.legislation.gov.uk/ukpga/2018/12/section/9/enacted
39 UK Government (2019). "The Online Pornography (Commercial Basis) Regulations 2019". www.legislation.gov.uk/uksi/2019/23/pdfs/uksi_20190023_en.pdf
40 www.bbfc.co.uk/
41 BBC News (2013). "Web porn: Just how much is there?". www.bbc.co.uk/news/technology-23030090
42 UK Government (2018). "Contingent Liability for the British Board of Film Classification (BBFC) as the Age Verification Regulator: Written Statement – HCWS986". www.parliament.uk/business/publications/written-questions-answers-statements/written-statement/Commons/2018-10-10/HCWS986/
43 Killock, J. (2019). "Jeremy Wright Needs to Act to Avert Disasters from Porn Age Checks". www.openrightsgroup.org/blog/2019/jeremy-wright-needs-to-act-to-avert-disasters-from-porn-age-checks
44 Wikipedia (n.d.). "Ashley Maddison Data Breach". https://en.wikipedia.org/wiki/Ashley_Maddison_data_breach
45 BBFC (2019). "Age-verification Certificate Standard". www.ageverificationregulator.com/assets/bbfc-age-verification-certificate-standard-april-2019.pdf

46 Martellozzo, E., Monaghan, A., Adler, J. R., Davidson, J., Leyva, R., & Horvath, M. A. H. (2016). "' … I wasn't sure it was normal to watch it … ' : A quantitative and qualitative examination of the impact of online pornography on the values, attitudes, beliefs and behaviours of children and young people." https://learning.nspcc.org.uk/media/1187/mdx-nspcc-occ-pornography-report.pdf
47 Phippen, A. (2017). "Children's Online Behaviour and Safety - Policy and Rights Challenges". Palgrave MacMillan.
48 UNICEF (2017). "Freedom of Expression, Association, Access to Information and Participation". www.unicef.org/csr/css/UNICEF_CRB_Digital_World_Series_EXPRESSION.pdf

4 Further progress in technological intervention
Knowing everything, always

In this chapter we delve further into the technology stack and consider the impact of other technological solutions on safeguarding scenarios, and also how legislation is perhaps not always the best place to provide requirements specifications. In the first part of the chapter we will look at the compliment to filtering – monitoring. The two are expected to work in tandem in schools, and we explore how they have evolved into what might be, by some, considered reassuring and necessary technology to ensure children and young people are safe, whereas others might see them more as impositions on privacy and civil liberties.

In extending the discussion to the other primary safeguarding tool to control access to inappropriate content, the chapter will go on to explore the nature of monitoring algorithms in content control, reflecting upon the basic techniques used (watch lists, keyword matching) initially but also considering how far monitoring, both in school and also in the home, can extend. For example, message interaction and sharing, the interception, interpretation, and redistribution of images, and elucidation of intent in communications based upon Natural Language Processing. The chapter questions whether the aims of the safeguarding approach can be realistically achieved through algorithms if the technology is poorly understood and not integrated into wider incident response mechanisms, and also whether monitoring is a technology for safety or control.

Monitoring has evolved from a school-centric technology to one that is also pervasive in the home and into the online familial ecosystem. And it is one that, as data would suggest in Chapter 2, is more likely to be used that blocking or filtering. The central concept of any monitoring approach is simple – collect data on online access at a network or application level, and develop response strategies accordingly.

The foundations of monitoring lie in similar data collection to filtering – keywords and URLs – although the response is different. As already illustrated in the case of the school who triggered a Prevent alert as a result of a young person accessing the UK Independence Party website, monitoring URLs and keywords is extremely viable technically. However, what the technology cannot do is develop an incident response following an alert – it can only match data with a watch-list and trigger an alarm. As with filtering, schools have an expectation under the Keeping Children Safe in Education statutory guidance[1] to have *appropriate* monitoring in place. And as with filtering, the guidance on what *appropriate* is is defined outside of the statutory instrument.

Within the school setting, the basic URL/keyword monitoring has now been superseded with other more active/pro-active platforms that can work at a far more sophisticated level. For example, being able to pro-actively monitor while a student is typing and making judgements on their intention as a result of this. The UK Safer Internet Centre guidance on "appropriate" monitoring[2] makes specific mention to the need for trained, knowable staff to respond to monitoring software alerts:

> Monitoring systems require capable and competent staff to sufficiently man-age them, together with the support and knowledge of the entire staff. Monitoring systems are there to safeguard children and the responsibility therefore should lie with the school leadership/governors and Designated Safeguarding Lead.

There is clear guidance that, within a school setting, the technology will not be an automated solution, but a tool to support staff in making safeguarding judge-ments. Which is, arguably, the best role for technology – to collect data, raise alerts, and leave decision-making to other stakeholders.

However, in recent years there has been significant evidence of feature creep in the monitoring system. While they used to function mainly around list-based interception and alerts, the technical capabilities of software and network systems means that the feature suite can now be far more complex. But, with the intro-duction of new features there seems to be little checking on whether, just because technology makes something possible, it *should* become part of a monitoring system. And there seems to be even less evidence of consideration of children's rights around these features and raises the questions – when does a monitor become surveillance, and did the child or their guardian consent to this?

Features in modern monitoring systems can be as wide-ranging as keystroke analysis (and keyword monitoring), live screen viewing, application monitoring and interception, real-time audio monitoring (listening in on a particular device in a classroom), and "evidence capture" features, which will collect data from the device (for example, image capture from the device's camera, screen grabs, and browsing history collection as a result of an alert). While all of these, to date, reside in the context of the school network and can arguably be justified as a result of the safeguarding duties of the school, there is historical evidence of inci-dents where monitoring software exceeding what is morally or legally acceptable. Perhaps the most famous case of this was in schools in the US, brought to light in the case *Robbins v. Lower Merion School District*[3].

This case has been subject to much discussion and it is worthwhile exploring the salient points to highlight the issue of technology extending moral bounda-ries. In this case, a number of schools in the Lower Merion School District in the US adopted a policy of providing students with laptops for both in school and at home use. While the expectation that the school might adopt a safeguarding approach that would use some forms of technology to monitor laptop usage is reasonable, and they need mitigate risk around the devices potentially being used for social or even illegal activities. However, the software the schools decided to install far exceeded this remit. As a result of one of the schools involved in the scheme disciplining a student for what they referred to as "inappropriate" behaviour at home, it was discovered that the laptops were not only monitoring internet access and application usage, but also sending a stream of images back to the school servers for analysis by staff. As a result of suspicions raised by Blake Robbins, the student being disciplined, it was finally determined that over 66,000 images of students at his school were collected via these devices using the built-in webcams on the laptops. As well as communicating images directly when an online connection was available, the monitoring software was also capable of collecting images locally and uploading them at a later time. While the school argued they had valid safeguarding reasons for collecting this data, it was clear from the case that consent had not been obtained, purpose specified, or expectations of data usage set. Even if there was a safeguarding concern, the fact that the image data was subsequently used in a student disciplinary, clearly demonstrated this remit had far been exceeded without fair consideration of the student's privacy or data-protection rights. Even if students had consented to data collected for safeguarding purposes, which is unlikely anyway, the use of this data for disciplinary purposes would far exceed this remit. Furthermore, it was argued that given the schools took a *pro-active* decision not to inform either students or parents of the installed monitoring software or request consent, there is evidence that the intention was covert and student's privacy had further been breached.

Unsurprisingly, the case found against the school district, and they were subject to a heavy fine. This case strongly highlights both the potential for abuse in a monitoring context with technology, and also the temptation to use this technology further than its intention. It would be doubtful that, for example, the software platform used would have been advertised as "collect images of children in their home and use this data to discipline them in school". However, given that functionality exists there is temptation to make use of the data available, regardless of data protection or sharing policies.

The case highlights what has already been illustrated in the UK Safer Internet Centre advice on monitoring – this is a system that requires not just technology, but also sound policy and well-trained staff. There is a risk with in-school monitoring technologies implemented without coherent and well-considered policy and incident response documents, young people can be treated very differently if alerts are raised, depending upon who was made aware of the alert and their own subjective judgement on what to do.

We need to bear in mind that, as discussed in Chapter 3, algorithms are not very good with the interpretation of context. Therefore, consider the scenario where a young person decides to search from something on an LGBTQ site related to gender and sexuality. We have seen from the Blocked project that many of these sites will be blocked, and we would expect some monitoring software to create alerts based upon these sites (particularly if using keyword-based strategies for identifying "inappropriate" content). If an alert is triggered, one would expect some sort of incident management process to commence. But how the incident is responded to would, we would suggest, be highly dependent upon the school. In this scenario it might be possible that the young person is using school systems because they do not wish their parents, who might be monitoring the internet access at home, to know they were searching for this information. If the school response to an alert is to bring in the parents, this might result in a very upsetting situation for the young person – this is hardly placing the welfare of the child at the heart of the safeguarding decision. While we would hope that each alert is dealt with in a pragmatic and student-centric manner, we can see from the Lower Merion case this is not always the reality of the situation.

While there are concerns about excessive monitoring and abuse of technology in schools there is at least reassurance that statutory instruments and legislation such as the GDPR means that there should be safeguards in place to ensure that inappropriate use and outright abuse of data might be controlled and even punished. However, this is not the case in the home setting.

We can see, from Chapter 2, that parents have many concerns related to their children and their online lives. Reflecting on the survey from Mumsnet we can see that over 50% of parents are concerned about:

- Being exposed to sexual imagery/pornography
- Bullying
- Being exposed to unpleasant or aggressive people (eg trolls, bad language)
- Being exposed to violent imagery
- Grooming
- Child sexual exploitation via video or photographs
- Deciding to meet strangers met online in real life
- Issues to do with body image and self-esteem
- Internet use interfering with sleeping patterns
- Being exposed to extremist attitudes

With this level of parental concern, it is understandable that they might be looking for tools or help to ensure their children are *safe* online. We can also see from the survey data that many are already using some level of technology in order to allay some of their fears. Against this concern, we are also seeing a burgeoning industry in safety apps, marketed against messages such as "ensuring peace of mind", "you will know that they are safe if you can see what they are doing", and "you will know they are safe if you know where they are". Within the online safety app marketplace there are all manner of functionalities offered:

- Filtering of "inappropriate content"
- Social media monitoring (both access, screen time and even what is being typed)
- Managing screen time through either reporting or pro-active management such as shutting the device down at given times or after a set duration)

- Managing screen time on specific apps or blocking them entirely
- Accessing messaging platforms so that parents can see messages sent
- Setting a block list in contact
- Seeing call logs
- Location tracking and "boundary setting" – being alerted if a child strays beyond set locations
- Alerting parents around sexual communication or cyberbullying
- Accessing images the child has taken to determine whether or not they are "appropriate"

We should bear in mind that these tools are proposed to address issues in ensuring a child is safe when they are online. There is, nevertheless, also a level of control in the use of some of these apps in the home, particularly around managing device time and access to a child's data. It is frequently suggested, such as in the Online Harms white paper, that parents need tools to ensure their children are not online excessively. However, there seems to be little understanding of what *excessive* means – it is an entirely arbitrary and subjective term. In more recent times, screen time has taken greater significance in the policy space due to concerns around the impact of screen time on young people's wellbeing.

In an interview in the *Times* on Saturday March 10 2018[4], the then Secretary of State for Digital, Culture, Media, and Sport, Matt Hancock, announced plans to bring in legislation that would restrict the amount of time children and young people could use social media platforms online in a simple soundbite:

> There is genuine concern about the amount of screen time young people are clocking up and the negative impact it might have on their lives. It is right that we think about what more we could do in this area.

The suggestion proposed a legal requirement for social media providers to put effective AV in place for anyone over the age of 13 (with the ill-informed belief that no children are on social media platforms before this age because its illegal) and to keep track of their usage, enabling legally defined limits of access to be put in place. We have already discussed the challenges of age verification for adults. For young people the age verification challenges are doubly difficult, given they are far less likely to have token-based forms of identification that prove their age to an online system.

Mr Hancock went on to state that, in an unsurprising sense of Deja vu:

> We are not afraid to legislate because it is our job to make sure laws are up to date.

Yet the evidence base around the relationship between young people's use of digital technology, the time they spend online, and its impact upon their wellbeing, is very immature and poorly understood. For a long time the American Association of Paediatrics (AAP) 2+2 guidance was viewed as a viable measure for screen time[5]. This simply stated, with little empirical evidence, that children under 2 should not be online at all, and those between the age of 2 and 16 should have a maximum of 2 hours. Arbitrary blanket measures fail to acknowledge the different types of screen time that can occur with young people – are we talking passive consumption (for example, watching a movie), single user interaction (for example, playing a game), multi-user interaction (for example, playing a game with friends), or something interactive and creative (for example, drawing a picture or producing a video). In a lot of the issues associated with online child safeguarding and protection, we may want simple answers when in reality it is not straightforward. While in recent times the AAP have revised this view to something more complex[6], the 2+2 is still often quoted.

Our own work with children and young people would suggest quite clearly that there is a *correlation* between the amount of time a child spends online and their exposure to risk[7]. We have seen from this large dataset that a child who spend a self-reported more than six hours a day online are twice as likely to have seen content or received comments that have upset them compared to someone who spends less than an hour online. It also shows that many young people who go online for over six hours a day are likely to do so because they are lonely. However, this is a correlation, not a causation and does not show whether children are lonely because they are online, or whether they are lonely, and therefore go online. Equally, we can see from our data that there are other heavy online users who are very happy (generally these would be self-disclosed gamers).

In a large 2017 study by Przbylski & Weinstein[8] of 120,000+ UK teens, the authors found that for 15-year-olds the effect of screen time on mental wellbeing depended on the category of screen time, and was different for weekdays and weekends. It also noted that clear negative associations with screen time were far smaller than, for example, positive associations between wellbeing and eating breakfast regularly. While young people might report on wellbeing issues we might relate to screen time, without exposure to a (probably unobtainable) full set of measures that might have an impact upon wellbeing we cannot confidently say that screen time is the causal negative factor. A more recent large-scale study by Orben & Przybylski[9] argued that their data (which was multinational and detailed) showed little evidence of a link between screen time and wellbeing.

Reflecting again on our own experiences talking to children and young people, we also see many positives for screen time. For some children, for example those in isolated communities, going online is a window to the wider world. For those wishing to explore sexuality and gender, in small communities finding peers is a challenge, whereas going online they can find many providing them with supportive, positive, and useful information. Coming out in a small town can still be challenging and has the potential to lead to serious physical harm for a young person. Being out online means they can talk with like-minded people without risk of being harmed by the less tolerant within their own communities.

For disabled children, being online might sometimes be a lifeline to an outside world. I can recall a young man with severe autistic traits telling me in the real world he was a coward but online he could be a hero – he loved to play Minecraft online with a large community of online friends for this reason. Those who struggle with direct contact with others, or who are near or completely non-verbal find an outlet for communication with online interaction. Those with physical disabilities might not be able to go out and socialise but they can do so online and it can be a highly positive impact upon their wellbeing. Is Mr Hancock really saying that the UK government knows better about how much time these children should spend online and how it would most positively impact upon their wellbeing than the children themselves or their parents?

Nevertheless, there are a number of monitoring solutions that provide parents with the means to control screen time on devices and, as we can see from the quote previous, there is political pressure that other providers *do more* to manage screen time. However, again, there seems to be little thought regarding the technical requirements to achieve this or the intrinsic complexity. While a political soundbite of "make sure children cannot be online for more than two hours a day" is simple to say, the reality of the complex relationship between young people and technology means this is, technically, more complex that the soundbite might imply. Firstly, there are potentially three ways to manage screen time – via application, device, or network. A lot of screen time apps work at a device level – for example, install the app onto a mobile device, and then manage screen time on it. The app may also have features such as application specific usage, or specific hours the device can be used for, but they will be limited to that specific device. If the young person, having run out of access time on Instagram on their mobile device, decided then to move to a laptop to access the platform via a web browser, the screen time management app would not be able to follow this.

At a network level, a router might provide access limitation across many devices but, again, they are challenges that would mean it could struggle to manage platform access on different devices using different means of application access. There are methods, at a network level, to deal with traffic from different apps – while all data will come down the same data connection (either a cable or a mobile connection), the network protocols allow a device to differentiate data, and tell it which app it needs to interact with, via *port* numbers. In theory, each type of network traffic (i.e. data going to different applications) will have a different port number. Therefore, a device could determine how long a session on a specific application would last by keeping track of the duration that data on a given port, or set of ports, is being communicated. For a game, such as Fortnite, where a lot of data is being communicated during play, this would be very easy to do. However, for social media platforms, this is not always the case, and all communication via a browser, regardless of platform, would come through the same ports. So, again, no solution.

There is one final approach to managing screen time – platform level control – moving the control of access away from the home into the hands of the platform provider. This is clearly the aim of Mr Hancock, given his threats to legislate if they fail to address this concern (which has virtually no evidence base to support). At a platform level, we can see a solution to one screen time problem – accessing a platform across multiple devices and applications (i.e. app or browser).

The platform provider themselves can monitoring time on the platform as a user-specific level, based upon a login, and can at least be aware of how long a young person (if they can accurately validate the age of the end user) has spent on their services. However, what this does not allow is an aggregate of time online *across* platforms. If Mr Hancock's threat of legislation is borne out, would the Government be asking platform providers to share access details on a young person with other, potentially competitive, services? Surely this would be a serious breach of a young person's rights to data protection? Given the importance placed on effective and proportionate data protection through the GDPR and Data Protection Act, we would hope that opposing legislation does not emerge that would expect to erode the young person's rights further, in order that they might be safeguarded? As we have already stated, this does not seem to be particularly well thought out. However, app providers can potentially build an effective business model on the back of a *reassurance myth* that will encourage parents to purchase their products, whether or not there is a real problem to solve.

Again, we are not stating, just as we were not saying children *should* be allowed free and unfettered access to pornography, that young people should be free to be online for as long as they wish, with no control over this. However, what we would take exception to is that technology has to provide the solution to this. Surely, a more realistic approach to excessive screen time is for a parent to manage it, through observation and house rules, rather than expecting technology to shut down a device for them after the application of a rule set that has little grasp of types of screen time, just minutes online and access across different port numbers (which only sort of analogises to specific applications).

Returning to the theme of this chapter, which very much centres around the feature creep in monitoring approaches, there are a number of issues arising from this list of solutions that cause concern beyond the current screen time debate. We have already discussed filtering at length, but the proposed functionality in the feature list of home monitoring solutions far outweighs proportionate response to child safeguarding concerns. It would seem that many parents, in order to reassure themselves that their children are safe, feel they need to know about every element of communication in their lives. We know, from many conversations with parents, that plenty believe it is their right to see every conversation their child has online and to know exactly who they are speaking to at any time. In order to ensure they are safe online, it is *essential* that parents can access all communications. This is the first generation where this has been possible – via technology. However, just because we can, is it acceptable that we do?

It would seem that we are confusing safety with surveillance, and because technology provides the methods to achieve this, we collect tool after tool that allows us to collect more and more data on our children – convinced with the notion that they are, in some way, safe if we have all of this data. However, as we point out frequently when delivering parents talks, what about those interactions that do not take place via a piece of technology? What about offline interactions? If the parent is concerned about their child being bullied, it is far more likely that this will occur in the school playground, and also far more likely that the child might come to physical harm as a result. There may be a view that in a playground situation there is a devolved monitoring responsibility on the part of school staff. However, one might also observe that one teacher in a playground with many children does not guarantee interception of harm. We have proposed, somewhat mischievously, that given the size and volume of storage available in mobile cameras now it is entirely possible to equip a child with such a device at the start of the school day and then when the child comes home the parent can play back their school day to ensure no harm has befallen them. In fact, with far greater capacity for data communications on modern mobile networks, it might, depending on local mobile coverage, be perfectly viable to live stream the child's day. It is an interesting test on how far a parent might wish to come in monitoring their child's behaviour. It would seem that such explicit monitoring is generally viewed as a step too far. And perhaps the *explicit nature* of the monitoring is also a factor that makes it less appealing – far better, instead, to monitor communications, social media posts, and internet access with less overt techniques, perhaps even techniques the child is not aware of, in order to reassure they are safe.

The concept of safety is interesting in this context – the justification for the use of increasingly oppressive monitoring is that it is needed to *assure* safety. In the same way that over-blocking is justified because it will *prevent* access to inappropriate content, and age verification will *stop* young people accessing pornography. Yet do these technologies do much to actually achieve safety? Will using these tools ensure a child is safe? Or are they tools to monitor and control behaviour instead, much like we say in the Lower Merion District case?

There are some risks that can be mitigated using this level of surveillance – for example the issues around grooming and contact from potential abusers might be mitigated by having access to contact lists and messaging. Yet these apps will only provide access to certain messaging platforms. While access to the mobile device's own telephony (i.e. calls and SMS) is relatively straightforward, to access app-specific messaging is more problematic, which is generally why only major platforms (for example Facebook, Instagram, Snapchat, Whatsapp) are covered.

And are the impacts on children's rights worthwhile? The impact does have some bearing on whether monitoring and tracking is performed in an overt or covert way. I have met parents in both camps – some will talk to their children about the tools they use, and the rationale for doing so. Some even allow their children to monitor and track their own use. Other parents will take a more meritocratic and covert perspective on the monitoring of their children's online lives, sometimes excused with the rationale that if the children know they are being monitored, they will modify their behaviour or find ways to bypass the tools.

One issue that is rarely raised, or the cause of challenge, as a result of these approaches to monitoring, is whether the parent is actually conducting illegal data collection activity on their child. The age of consent for children to be capable of consenting to their data being collected, and therefore being responsible for their own data, is defined in the Data Protection Act 2018 as 13. This is the age that the Office of the Information Commissioner state that children are capable of exercising their own data protection rights, on their own behalf[10].

While this has not be tested in case law, we might theorise that is a parent does not have consent from their teenaged child to collect personal, and potentially sensitive, data about them, they could be illegally processing and storing that data.

Monitoring does raise some interesting tensions between safeguarding and children's rights. Regardless of the approach, there are some very real impacts on privacy in particular as a result of these tools, but also on rights such as freedom of expression and access to the media and, in the case of *covert* monitoring, placing a significant restriction on respecting the views of the child. By way of illustration, a recent BBC News report[11] had a parent justifying their own approach to the question they had posed of "So how can we keep them safe from harmful content?". It seems, in the case of this article (and this resonates with our own conversations with some parents), it to look at everything they do online:

> My two daughters, aged 11 and 13, loudly protest about 'violations of privacy' when they realised I could see every site and app they've visited.
> Once I've reassured them that this is not about snooping, but more about limitation and safety, they grudgingly seem to accept the new controls.

We see this tension between surveillance and security discussed in many layers of society. As well as young people, there is always public debate around the right to encryption whenever a terrorist incident with some link to encrypted communications[12] arises, whether facial recognition is a valid tool to use in public events[13] or whether the UK's high levels of closed-circuit television camera surveillance is justified[14].

French philosopher Michel Foucault's work on discipline and punishment[15] has frequently been drawn upon when considering the role of surveillance technologies in modern society[16]. In particular, Foucault's interpretation of Bentham's physical Panopticon – the architectural prison structure where the inmate can see nothing but the means of their own surveillance, whereas the controlling sentinel can observe everything the inmate does[17].

Foucault observes that in such a system, the subject of the surveillance becomes

the object of information, never a subject in communication.

If the child is the object of information, imposed with such stringent monitoring and surveillance technologies, using the excuse that "we need to see everything you do to ensure that you are safe"[18] we are potentially imposing an unacceptable level of control and data collection upon them because what we are actually wishing to achieve is not safe children, but compliant ones. They are observed, with no power to prevent this, and play no part in the surveillance scenario, other than providing the observer with information about their behaviour. The Panopticon asserts the *automatic functioning of power* where the subject knows they are being watched, but can do nothing about it. In a scenario where a parent can *see everything* related to a child's online life *always*, we are experiencing the application of a *digital panopticon* where the child is the object of information and the parent is the observer. With the application of technology that proposes that a parent can see every communication, image, or keystroke on a device, while they might justify this surveillance as a means to reassure themselves that this is the only way the child will be kept safe, we are establishing power imbalance that has long been viewed as a model of control.

The approach seems utterly disproportionate to the task in hand. While we can appreciate parental concern and the lack of pragmatic advice in this area can sometimes lead to rash decisions (see Chapter 6 when we discuss *Momo week*), we need to appreciate that these organisations are providing these tools as a commercial transaction. There is money to be made from parental fear, yet we still see little evidence that a lot of these tools provide the safety that parents crave[19].

The tools provided undoubtedly have some uses in allowing a child to be monitored and mitigate risk, but they will certainly not keep them safe, and this highlights a problematic issue with the discourse in this area. If our goal is to ensure children and young people are safe online, and implement this with technologies that will ensure safety, we will fail, as we will never guarantee safety online. There will always be risks, in the same way that there will always be hazards for children and young people in the physical world.

This is perhaps highlighted most keenly with the growing use of Global Position System (GPS) tracking technology implemented in either dedicated physical devices (such as trackable wristbands) or as a function of a mobile device. We are speaking to increasing numbers of children and young people who have some level of tracking by their parents. While techniques might differ, the premise is the same – the parent will install an app, or enable a tracking function on a device, which allows them to see where the child is, generally via mapping software. Additionally, there might also be alerts raised if a child strays outside of geographical locations (for example, a school). In general, those children who are being tracked that we have spoken to are fairly accepting of it – they feel it keeps their parents reassured that they are safe, and they do not feel it restricts their own behaviour.

However, peers will generally be more concerned and, in general, pleased that they are not subjected to such surveillance (or aware that they are). It is interesting too, to note that among students at universities, we see that there are many students who are accepting of tracking by partners. With such emergent technology, it is difficult to make any inferences around whether those comfortable being tracked by partners were also tracked by parents, but there is a growing social acceptance that, given the technology exists, why should we not use it? Yet we must, once again, reflect upon whether the safeguarding justification for the use of such technology is borne out in the actual application.

We were recently party to a somewhat bizarre story of a parent upset with their 17-year-old daughter who had claimed to be visiting a (female) friend when she was actually at her boyfriend's house. The parents were conflicted because, while annoyed that their daughter had lied to them, they felt powerless to deliver any form of punishment. When asked why they could not punish their daughter they said that their daughter was not aware she was being tracked and if they were to tell her off then she would realise this is happening. This peculiar impasse highlighted a dichotomy between safety and control. Were these parents tracking their daughter (covertly) because they were concerned about her, or were they doing it because it gave them some level of power and control over her? There was no suggestion that her being at her boyfriend's house was making her unsafe, there was more annoyance than concern, and this arose because she had lied to them (perhaps because she knew she would be told she wasn't allowed to go to her boyfriend's house?). It would certainly seem in this scenario that there was no worry regarding their daughter's safety, but an annoyance that she had chosen not to tell them where she was going. And the wish that they had decided, in the balance, that further convert tracking was preferable to making her aware her being tracked, did demonstrate some problematic attitudes in the familial relationship.

In another discussion with an early years practitioner, we were told that at the end of a typical morning session at the practitioner's setting, a parent commented that she was disappointed to observe that the children had not been taken outside until mid-morning on such a lovely sunny day. When the practitioner asked the parent how she knew this, she said her child wore a trackable device which she monitored at home. Again, a safeguarding justification for the use of this technology seems tenuous. The child is in a secure setting with trained professionals within an *in loco parentis* relationship. Given the physical security of the setting, alongside the policies in place to manage the arrival and collection of children, it was arguably a more secure environment than a child at home. Yet the parent still felt the need to reassure themselves that the child was safe and, as it turned out, use the technology to make judgements on practice within the setting. While safeguarding might have been the façade, the technology was clearly being used to monitoring not only the child but the setting too. As a result of this incident, the setting now has a policy that trackable devices are left at the door when the child arrives in the morning.

It is interesting to note that recent guidance from the UK Sentencing Council[20] has begun to explicitly refer to GPS tracking as evidence of coercion and control in relationships and in a domestic abuse case it might be used as a justification for a harsher sentence. Yet there are some who see it as perfectly reasonable to track their children as a reassurance that they are safe (and arguably so they have control over their movements and can use the data collected as a means for discipline). The UK celebrity Jamie Oliver recently promoted[21] the use of tracking technology, saying it was a "brilliant" way to ensure his children were safe when they were away from the family home.

Yet is this an illusion of safety, and arguably the justification for more power and control in the parental relationship? While we might acknowledge the fears many parents have around child abduction, would this technology prevent this from happening? The technology does not show where the child is, it shows where their *device* is. Someone wishing to abduct a child is likely to be knowledgeable around the fact that devices can be tracked, and could dispose of them in the event of an abduction. Moreover, if a parent is monitoring their child remotely, watching a dot move around a map, the physical distance means that the safeguarding reassurance is entirely hollow. If, for example, the child was 40 miles away, and then the blinking dot on the map began to accelerate further from the home location, how might the parent address this safety concern? Perhaps the first response might be to call the child, but what would then happen if the child did not answer. Would the next phase of this scenario be contacting law enforcement to say that their child is too far away or, in the event of the dot disappearing completely, missing?

While there are some scenarios where it would seem proportionate to use tracking technology in a positive manner, for example where a child might suffer from a medical condition such as epilepsy where they might suffer from blackouts. In this case, the tracking technology might actually be empowering – they gain a certain level of freedom by being able to be away from the family home, and all parties are comfortable in the knowledge that in the event of seizure, the young person could be located.

However, this technology is also applied far too easily in the familial relationship as a safeguarding measure with sinister undertones – "we love you, therefore we need to track you". Again, this is another technology where the façade of safeguarding can be used to exert more control over the child – as can be seen in the example previous, the concern was not because the parents felt their daughter was unsafe, but anger because she had disobeyed them. And the risk of exposure to this tracking, and perhaps the then subsequent withdrawal of the technology (if the daughter in our example, quite correctly, might take exception to being covertly tracked) meant that the control the parents thought they obtained through the technology could not be realised as punishment.

Foucault defined the concept of the *Docile Body*[22] as

> one that may be subjected, used, transformed, and improved. And that this docile body can only be achieved through strict regimen of disciplinary acts.

In essence, a malleable object on which disciplinary force is acted in order that it might be controlled, and therefore more useful to those who hold power. After all, a docile body is less likely to challenge authority or disobey. He referred to the role of observation and surveillance in the achievement of the docile body within 18th-century military structures:

> In the perfect military camp, all power would be exercised solely through exact observation; each gaze would form a part of the overall functioning of power.

and explored the role of technology in achieving this:

> side by side with the major technology of the telescope, the lens and the light beam, which were an integral part of the new physics and cosmology,

there were the minor techniques of multiple and intersecting observations, of eyes that must see without being seen; using techniques if subjugation and methods of exploitation, an obscure art of light and the visible was secretly preparing a new knowledge of man.

It is interesting to reflect upon what Foucault might have made of the modern technologies used to keep children safe (at least this is the argument for deploying them). While he was referring to physical surveillance, unseen but with the subject aware of its existence, the digital world provides far greater depth of both overt and convert surveillance of children and young people. Clearly, the examples given previously were not about keeping a child safe, they were technologies used to know where they are, and whether they were being compliant (docile?). In 1978, the psychologist Jack Flasher coined the term "Adultism"[23], to refer to the prejudice adults can exert on children from a position of privilege and judgement, to challenge their worldview because it is different to their own while having the requisite power (financial, legislative, physical, etc.) to restrict young people's lives. We see adultist elements in both the online safeguarding policy space and also the responses of other stakeholders to keep children "safe".

The cybersecurity expert Bruce Schneier, in 2006, observed the impact of surveillance on the population as a whole:

> For if we are observed in all matters, we are constantly under threat of correction, judgment, criticism, even plagiarism of our own uniqueness. We become children, fettered under watchful eyes, constantly fearful that – either now or in the uncertain future – patterns we leave behind will be brought back to implicate us, by whatever authority has now become focused upon our once-private and innocent acts. We lose our individuality, because everything we do is observable and recordable.[24]

If one is already a child, and is subject to such high and visible levels of surveillance, one can only assume even greater docility as a result. There is, however, a fundamental flaw in this digital panopticon. Unlike the physical panopticon, where the structures of the environment mean the observed is powerless, this is not the case in the online world. Those who wish to control need to bear in mind that the digital panopticon is easier to break out of than the physical one. Our conversations with young people would highlight that if they know they are being monitored, they will attempt to circumvent this (as reflected in over 50% of young people even in year 4 saying they can get around "some" of the house rules put in place). They will find ways to do this, whether this will be using a different device, making use of proxying or encryption, or even something as simple as switching the device off (in the case of being aware they are being tracked). While the information, and power imbalance, is afforded to the parent by the tools at their disposal, the knowledge gap that exists between child and parent can also be disproportionate, and therefore young people will find ways to bypass the constraints imposed upon them.

Our faith in code to be the "solution" is allowing us to blindly erode a child's rights and, in some cases, encourage them into more risky behaviour, because technology is proposed that will allay our fears. However, there is a lack of criticality in determining their capabilities, in part because there is no transparency in the functionalities of the algorithms themselves. If vendors purport a piece of functionality, we have no means to check whether this is actually the case. So vendors tell us that these technologies will make our children safe, and we will believe it because it fits into our need to *do more* to safeguard them without having to engage in more complex discourse around discussion or negotiation – the tools guarantee safety, so we don't have to.

One aspect of the monitoring toolkit we have not explored in detail is the growing body of apps that claim to perform some form of image recognition – an app that will sit on the child's device and ensure they cannot send indecent images they have taken. These algorithms, as already touched upon, will generally have some element of *artificial intelligence* about it or, more correctly *machine learning* (given there is little actual intelligence, more evolutionary decision-making based upon data available). This will be the focus of Chapter 5, which looks at the final class of technologies, and the current discourse that machine learning will be able to solve all of the safeguarding problems we hope code can resolve for us.

Notes

1 UK Government (2018). "Keeping Children Safe in Education – Statutory Guidance For Schools and Colleges". https://assets.publishing.service.gov. uk/government/uploads/system/uploads/attachment_data/file/741314/ Keeping_Children_Safe_in_Education__3_September_2018_14.09.18.pdf
2 UK Safer Internet Centre (n.d.). "Appropriate Monitoring". www.saferinternet. org.uk/advice-centre/teachers-and-school-staff/appropriate-filtering-and-moni-toring/appropriate-monitoring
3 PacerMonitor (n.d.). "*Robbins V Lower Merion District*". www.pacermonitor. com/view/6LZS7RA/ROBBINS_et_al_v_LOWER_MERION_SCHOOL_ DISTRICT_et__paedce-10-00665__0001.0.pdf
4 *The Times* (2018). "Time Limits For Children Hooked on Social Media". www.thetimes.co.uk/article/time-limits-for-children-hooked-on-social-media-3s66vwgct
5 Graber, D. (2015). "Screen Time and Kids: Pediatricians Work on a New Prescription". www.huffingtonpost.com/diana-graber/screen-time-and-kids-pedi_b_8224342.html
6 American Academy of Paediatrics (2016). "American Academy of Paediatrics Announces New Recommendations for Children's Media Use". www.aap.org/ en-us/about-the-aap/aap-press-room/pages/american-academy-of-pediatrics-announces-new-recommendations-for-childrens-media-use.aspx
7 Phippen (2018). "Young People, Internet Use and Wellbeing; A Report Series – Screentime". https://swgfl.org.uk/assets/documents/young-people-internet-use-and-wellbeing.pdf
8 Przybylski, A. K. & Weinstein, N. (2017). "A large-scale test of the goldilocks hypothesis: Quantifying the relations between digital-screen use and the mental well-being of adolescents". *Psychological Science*, 28(2), 204–215.

9 Orben, A. & Przybylski, A. K. (2019). "Screens, Teens, and Psychological Well-Being: Evidence From Three Time-Use-Diary Studies". *Psychological Science*, 30(5), 682–696.

10 Office of the Information Commissioner (n.d.). "What Rights Do Children Have?". https://ico.org.uk/for-organisations/guide-to-data-protection/guide-to-the-general-data-protection-regulation-gdpr/children-and-the-gdpr/what-rights-do-children-have/

11 BBC News (2019). "Rape Victims Among Those to Be Asked to Hand Phones to Police". www.bbc.co.uk/news/uk-48086244

12 UK government (2017). "Encryption and Counter-Terrorism: Getting the Balance Right". www.gov.uk/government/speeches/encryption-and-counter-terrorism-getting-the-balance-right

13 Big Brother Watch (2018). "Face Off – The Lawless Growth of Facial Recognition in UK Policing". https://bigbrotherwatch.org.uk/wp-content/uploads/2018/05/Face-Off-final-digital-1.pdf

14 Surveillance Camera Commissioner (2017). "Annual Report 2016/17 – Presented to Parliament Pursuant to Section 35(1)(b) of the Protection of Freedoms Act 2012". https://assets.publishing.service.gov.uk/government/uploads/system/uploads/attachment_data/file/672286/CCS207_CCS0118716124-1_Annex_A_-_AR_2017-_web.pdf

15 Foucault, M. (1975). *Discipline and Punish*. A. Sheridan, Tr., Paris, Gallimard.

16 Boyle, J. (2017). Foucault in cyberspace: Surveillance, sovereignty, and hardwired censors. In *Law and Society Approaches to Cyberspace* (pp. 235–263). Routledge.

17 Leaton Gray, S. and Phippen, A. (2017). *Invisibly Blighted*. UCL Press.

18 An advertising strapline by one of these providers is the somewhat chilling "See everything. Always".

19 Przybylski, A. K., and Nash, V. "Internet filtering technology and aversive online experiences in adolescents". *The Journal of Pediatrics*, 184.

20 Sentencing Council (2018). "Overarching Principles: Domestic Abuse Definitive Guideline". www.sentencingcouncil.org.uk/wp-content/uploads/Overarching-Principles-Domestic-Abuse-definitive-guideline-Web.pdf

21 Petter, O. (2018). "Jaime Oliver Reveals He Tracks Daughter's Location on App – But Parenting Experts Say it Could Cause Future Problems". www.independent.co.uk/life-style/health-and-families/jamie-oliver-tracks-location-life360-kids-parenting-a8545136.html

22 Foucoult, M. (1975). *Discipline and Punish*. A. Sheridan, Tr., Paris, Gallimard.

23 Flasher, J. (1978). Adultism. *Adolescence*, 13(51), 517–523.

24 Schneier, B. (2016). "The Eternal Value of Privacy". www.wired.com/2006/05/the-eternal-value-of-privacy

5 Algorithmic approaches to tackling online safeguarding

In this chapter we focus specifically on classes of technological intervention, we explore what might be considered the state of the art – namely machine learning and intelligent systems that are proposed to provide solutions to issues that have long plagued the safeguarding arena, for example, image recognition and natural language processing. Alongside consideration of these technologies and what they are *realistically* capable of, we will also examine whether their use is ethical and proportionate, or whether an overreliance on opaque technologies is perhaps not the best future for online safeguarding. Future directions are considered as well as the implications of algorithms in this problem space long term.

A common emerging thread among the new class of online safeguarding tools for both home use and also specialist domains such as law enforcement is they generally claim some form of artificial intelligence (AI). While AI techniques are increasingly applied in complex problem spaces that require some level of intelligence, the chapter will reflect upon the potential risk associated with techniques whose outputs might elicit effective results but whose internal functionality are often poorly understood by both system developers and users, and therefore may result in outcomes that might be misinterpreted or poorly understood while the systems continue to "learn" from the data they are fed. We have embarked on this discussion in Chapter 4 by exploring the purported functionality by home monitoring solutions that will report alerts to parents if the child is being bullied on their device, or groomed, self-generated an indecent image of themselves, or received such an image to their device. Or, more accurately, when the system decides that such an event has occurred.

We have discussed, at length, the role keyword matching plays in filtering and monitoring systems, and these behavioural identification systems when monitoring textual communication, will adopt a similar model at their core with some form of *inference engine* to attempt to determine the context of the communication (for example, is a message "you're such a slut" a banterous exchange between peers, or an attempt grooming by a predatory adult). The majority of *intelligence* applied to these scenarios will generally (for example[1,2,3]) be based upon a model that will involve:

- Acquisition of sample of abuse from <social media platform>
- Categorisation of samples by human researchers to determine/classify whether phrases in the sample were <type of abuse being explored>

- Identify suitable classification system to be used to develop predictive model for identification of <type of abuse being explored>
- Train classification system with <x%> of sample so classifier can "identify" examples of <type of abuse being explored>
- Load <y% of sample> into classifier system to determine whether the classifier correctly identifies <type of abuse being explored>
- Present results
- Refine and improve results based upon types of classifier and larger and better classified data sets
- Repeat

We can see this approach in the literature for at least the last ten years and it is an entirely valid body of knowledge related to approaches for the identification of text-based abuse. However, results will vary based upon types of machine learning used, selection of samples, categorisation of samples, size of samples, volume of training data, and so on. They are typically, unsurprisingly, also fairly small in sample size (for example, a few thousand comments) compared to large scale commercial systems which will be processing millions of communications per day.

It is more difficult, therefore, to determine approaches used in commercial systems due to the volume of data and also because techniques used will rarely be disclosed in any technical level of detail. However, given operation and efficacy it is reasonable to assume that similar approaches are being used given the reporting from the larger organisations. Facebook, for example, recently produced a press article on their suicide detection "AI"[4] that made it very clear they were using weighted keyword terms within a classifier system, alongside training data sets, in order to make judgements on the possibility that someone might be expressing suicidal ideation. We have already seen attempts to move these algorithms into the production environment with varying degrees of success[5] and also some legislative challenges[6].

Returning to one of the central premises of this text –if policy makers do not understand technology, they will never implement effective legislation and consequently emergent technologies will be subject to poor requirement specification and even expectation. However intelligent these algorithms are, they will only ever be as smart as the people who write them and the data they are fed. They are not perfect, objective arbiters of morality, they are interpreters of data, making decisions based upon the data they have fed into them, with a rules base coded into them, as explored in great detail in Cathy O'Neil's *Weapons of Math Destruction*[7]. As such, they can only ever understand new data in the context of data they have already been shown. They cannot make inference to contexts and information that have not been presented to them, and the learning is entirely dependent on the training data.

A deeper philosophical question exists around the application of systems to interpret human behaviours and make judgements based upon data provided (for example, comments on a social media post). There have been calls for "grooming detection algorithms"[8] to be implemented in social media platforms. This might sound impressive in a soundbite, but there is a risk of defamation due to the technical complexities in implementing such an approach. While there is academic research in such algorithms[9,10,11], in these cases small datasets (compared to a production environment) and pre-classified data (i.e. the data being fed into the system is noted as grooming discourse) still elicit results that would suggest deployment in a production environment would risk an unacceptable level of false positives. If a platform provider was to collect this data based upon a false positive and make unfounded accusation, there might be severe repercussions for the organisation. While these are useful tools to support human operators, the expectation of automation of these complex scenarios, without sufficient trailing in production systems, is concerning.

By way of illustration, another recent press report[12] hinted at similar approaches being used at Twitter for a very different type of harmful content – terrorist materials. While Twitter has been very successful at the removal of Islamist terrorist content, they struggle more with other forms of extremist content such as white supremacist and far-right rhetoric. The argument presented by Twitter was that *aggressive* blocking of Islamist content is generally accepted by their user base. They are more likely to accept over-blocking of this sort of material, and will be more effectively policed by the community (i.e. posts are more likely to be reported) than that related to far-right extremism. Furthermore, if they attempted to aggressively block far-right content, with a keyword focus, there was a likelihood, it was claimed, that right-wing politicians and even the US president Donald Trump might be subject to blocks.

The community around far-right rhetoric is far more ambiguous, and the platform risk alienating some parts of it with strong control of this content (the far right is a particularly vociferous domain for freedom of speech arguments[13]). The article also raised an interesting, more complex, question around content moderation regarding whether this is a purely technical challenge for platform providers, or whether social norms have to play a role in the moderation. Which, conversely, has implications for policy where the platform provider is seen as the only stakeholder with any responsibility for content control.

Image and video-recognition algorithms, as applied in the policing of online child sexual exploitation and image recognition in app-based monitoring systems, will sometimes adopt a similar approach but, obviously, have a larger data processing load, given the complexity of the data within an image, compared to textual data.

Image recognition in algorithmic form is not really image recognition as we might interpret from a human perspective at all. A long-established approach, as discussed in Chapter 3, draws upon hashing technology already discussed to successfully identify reposted images that have already been classified and hashed by hashing the unidentified image. We have already discussed that, within the confines of the technology solution, this is an approach that works, because it is a harmonious relationship between human moderator and the use of algorithms to do what algorithms do best – processing data and pattern matching. These algorithms are good at processing an image into a hash once it has been judged illegal by a moderator. All the "recognition" algorithm is doing is taking an image, applying the same hash function, and if the hash value matches. It has no knowledge of whether the image is indecent, it is just following the rules defined by its code and doing an equivalence test. There is nothing in this technology that currently supports the identification of new indecent images, or makes inferences of indecency in relation to new, previously unseen content. The algorithm can merely confirm whether the image is the same as a known image, previously identified as indecent through human intervention. There is no intelligence, it is simply data matching.

The other class of image recognition attempts to carry out a similar function to the textual detection approaches discussed previously. These statistical or machine-learning approaches adopt a more predictive solution which, for the purposes of detecting indecent images of children, applies mathematical techniques to identify common characteristics in a set of images (or increasingly, video). Again, this approach is based upon the data in the image (for example, the proximity of different colour pixels to each other, the frequency of images of different colours, specific colours in specific parts of the image, etc.). More recently[14] artificial intelligence (AI) techniques have been applied as an alternative approach to identify common characteristics within candidate child exploitation images entered into a detection system. Nonetheless, these techniques do little to understand the meaning of the image; rather they identify similar characteristics within the data held in the image – in much the same way that a textual processing system would function, the algorithm is loaded with a set of known images and told "find images with a similar data composition to these".

With statistical and AI-based techniques in this domain, the recognition component still resides in comparing a data artefact with others to identify similarity, using probabilistic methods to make an estimation of similarity and, within thresholds, report on a match. No inference is made by the algorithm concerning the meaning of the candidate image, just whether the image is a statistical relative of other images that have had similar techniques applied to them. Generally, machine-learning algorithmic approaches rely on being *trained* in the same way as natural language systems used for text processing – they are fed collections of pre-classified images (in the case of sexual or indecent images, the images would have already been classified by human intervention) to look for data similarities and make predictions, so that when an unknown image is submitted to the learning system, it can make an estimate of the similarity of the image to the training set, with thresholds set to what would be an acceptable match. However, this is an estimate based on similarity, of data in the files, not a similarity of the meaning of the image or a neural interpretation of what is represented in the image. Two indecent images may appear very different in their composition, and whereas we, as humans, will recognise both as indecent (within our own interpretation of what indecency is), algorithms are unable to make such an inference based on an assessment of the physical properties of an image alone. Therefore, while such systems could be trained with a set of indecent images of children such that there might be a likelihood that statistically similar images will be found, this does not mean that such a system would be able to identify *all* indecent images of children, again, just those that have similarity to the training sets will be identified. For example, there is also a risk that indecent images of children might share characteristics with adult pornography, and there might be statistical or inferred matches with this type of content.

There is an apocryphal tale often told about an image detection system that tried to detect tanks hidden in cover such as trees. While it has been debunked[15] it is a worthwhile illustration of the issues between believing an algorithm achieves one's aims (the unconscious bias in user acceptance) and actually understanding the function of the algorithm in a logical and transparent manner. The story, which has many variations, purports that an image detection algorithm was developed to correctly identify the difference between a tree, and a tank hiding behind a tree, on the battlefield. In a test environment, after the algorithm had been "trained" with 100 test images, half trees, half tress with tanks hiding behind them, and told which they were, the algorithm would successfully identify an image with near perfect precision – that is, it would be able to tell the difference between a tree and a tank hiding behind a tree with a new image. However, when deployed in a live system the detection went down to the equivalence of a random match. When the failure of the system was explored forensically, it turned out that all of the training images of trees without tanks were taken on sunny days, and all of those with tanks in the image were taken on cloudy days. The algorithm was actually, very accurately, performing the match based upon the weather, rather than the objects in the image.

While this story has become something of an urban myth, image recognition scholars have acknowledged its viability. Given that most image recognition algorithms recognise based upon the data properties of the image, rather than what the image represents in semantic terms (which is, of itself, extremely difficult to do algorithmically for reasons discussed previously), and largely rely on training sets to recognise comparable images, the identification of unknown images, which we might argue a new indecent image always would be, is far more complex.

Even the most advanced algorithms in this field have acceptance rates that would struggle to be termed reliable without some form in human intervention. In a recent blog post on Algorithmia[16] around an advanced "nudity detection" algorithm (note the significance here that this was nudity, rather than indecency) the testers returned a maximum positive accuracy of 83.64% and maximum negative accuracy of 87%. Therefore, in over 1 in 10 cases, the algorithm would not be able to accurately detect whether an image contained naked skin, let alone whether the image was indecent or a scene of abuse. In order for such techniques to scale to meet the challenge of the identification of indecent images of minors, we require levels of accuracy much greater than many state-of-the-art detection algorithms allow. While more recent artificial intelligence tools for the identification of new, previously unseen child exploitation media files report accuracy rates higher than this for image and video detection[17] such approaches have not been applied to the task of detecting newly produced, sexual content involving children and young people.

Even though the literature does little to demonstrate the effectiveness of image recognition in open social contexts and broad recognition criteria, this does not stop either vendors or politicians from purporting these intelligent algorithms being the next big thing in online safeguarding. Vendor claims that a parent can know "whenever your child takes an indecent selfie" have created a marketplace for safeguarding software that aims to reassure parents that their children are prevented from engaging in the exchange of indecent, self-generated, images. While some send suspect image sent from the child's phone to the parent's own device, others claim advanced image recognition capabilities, and the ability to reliably identify everything from indecency to self-harm. Several such products offer a range of functionalities, such as alerting the parent when such an image is generated, forwarding the image to the parent, or posting a warning on the child's phone about a suspect image. While there is little scrutiny of these products and their purported functionality, there are claims of high degrees of accuracy and very low false positives rates.

However, is it any wonder that vendors are implementing and marketing these solutions given that policy direction is heading this way? Let us consider the proposal of the then British Health Secretary Jeremy Hunt, who while giving evidence to a Health Select Committee hearing on suicide prevention, said the following[18]:

> I just ask myself the simple question as to why it is that you can't prevent the texting of sexually explicit images by people under the age of 18, if that's a lock that parents choose to put on a mobile phone contract. Because there is technology that can identify sexually explicit pictures and prevent it being transmitted.

Within this simple paragraph, we have much to unpack when considering whether this proposed technological solution is actually viable.

First, the assurance that any child will be on a contract where the parents can set up the device so the service provider recognises the end user as a minor is somewhat naïve. There are a wealth of reasons this might not be the case, such as phones passed from different family members, phones inherited from friends, a device that does not run a sim, instead, will just use WiFi connectivity instead, "pay as you go" phones where there are less precise checks on the age of the end user (particularly if the parent is purchased by the parents for a child), and the more fundamental issue that even if a parent does add a child's phone onto their contract (for example), this does not necessarily mean that the device will be registered as a device for a minor (it is up to the parent to specify this). Given there are no other means for age verification (at the current time) of a specific device use in a multiple device contract, there might be many reasons why the service provider cannot confidently authenticate that the device belongs to a minor in the first place.

If we assume, for the sake of argument, we can determine that the device user is a minor, our next challenge is what does Mr Hunt actually mean by transmission. A quick check of one of the author's devices suggests messaging potential using MMS, WhatsApp, Facebook Messenger, email, Gmail, Bluetooth file exchange, Twitter messaging, Instagram messaging, cloud-based shared storage, LinkedIn messaging, or the device's own proprietary data transfer protocols. All of these apps are capable of sending an image to a recipient (or group of recipients in some cases). Is Mr Hunt suggesting that each one of these apps needs to implement their own "technology that can identify sexually explicit pictures and prevent it being transmitted" or is he suggesting that perhaps this is a piece of technology that the phone provider implements and in some way integrates into the functionality of the application level software? And what if one was to add a new app to my device? Should any new app with file sharing capability also implement this technology? Surely this would be an impossible burden on any application developer?

However, perhaps the more problematic part of his statement is that he claims there is technology that exists that can identify a sexually explicit image. A fundamental concern with this statement is there is no clear, legally agreed, definition for what *sexually explicit* is. While we do have a clear definition in the statute for extreme pornography[19] and even, arguably, pornography (as discussed in Chapter 3), sexually explicit is a far more ambiguously defined concept. And as we have already discussed, algorithms are very poor at ambiguity. If we are to apply generic machine learning to Mr Hunt's, apparently established, technology, we need to train the algorithm with data defined as sexually explicit by *someone*. We have already determined that there is no universally accepted definition for sexually explicit so we would have to add another layer of ambiguity by having subjective judgements on an image set by a human, or group of humans, who will determine whether or not an image is suitable for the training data by deeming it sexually explicit.

Furthermore, what Mr Hunt is referring to here is the detection of sexually explicit images of minors – given he is proposing this as a solution to prevent young people from sending these images (because he claims this is one of the reasons young people have mental health issues). Therefore, in order to train an algorithm to identify newly generated sexually explicit images of a minor, the data set needs to comprise of sexually explicit images of children. This places an unreasonable and potentially illegal burden on the technology provider – even possession of an image outside of a law enforcement arena would mean the company was breaking the law (in the UK – the Protection of Children Act 1978). To expect an organisation to keep a training set of sexually explicit images of minors would be extremely concerning, and goes some way to explaining why such technologies do not exist. However, evidence from a Secretary of State carries weight, and will result in other stakeholders believing that this technology is readily available, which will then create greater public dissatisfaction because the sector is not implementing something they have been told is available, even if it is not. Which leads the technology sector to develop nearest fit technologies that do not do what is expected, but something that is in the same ballpark. Which, of course, does nothing to solve the problems these solutions are supposed to tackle.

However, there is a more fundamental, philosophical issue at work here too – Mr Hunt appears to be asking the technology sector to create technology that would sit on a child's mobile device and make moral judgements on the nature of the images the child has taken, and control the communications of these images as a result. Surely, this extends the role of the technology provider beyond what is both ethical and socially acceptable? Should we really be expecting private sector organisations making decisions about censorship on a citizen's mobile device based upon an ideology? We have, through this text, discussed the rights of the child being central to the developing narrative around the use of algorithms in online child protection and safeguarding and fundamental to this is the erosion of children's privacy at the expense of their safeguarding.

Given the limitations to the accuracy of image recognition algorithms described previously, we would be concerned about the rights and wellbeing of children and families if algorithms were applied as the "solution" to this issue, as called for by Mr Hunt. Should we be happy, even with the rates of sensitivity and specificity maintained by more advanced nudity detection algorithms cited previously, that over 1 in 10 children could be falsely implicated in the self-generation of nude images, and that the result of this detection could be an alert to their parents? A false positive could result in intra-familial distress, conflict and the kinds of sanctions children so often report they fear, for example, a parent demanding access to, or confiscating, their phone when no such sanctions were necessary. With software that simply forwards all images onto the parent's phone without the knowledge or consent of the child, this should be framed as a severe challenge to the child's privacy. Safeguarding should not replace children's rights, yet we seem to think that it is a price worth paying if a child is kept "safe". Even though we struggle to appreciate what safe looks like, or even if these apps do actually safeguard. As we have already discussed previously, a lot of the functionality offered seems to have more to do with control and discipline than safeguarding.

In this scenario we are expecting an algorithm to reside on a child's mobile device and monitor their behaviours and make moral judgements. As we have already discussed, subjective concepts such as morality are very difficult to implement in code, particularly without legislative foundation. Moreover, does the fact that a piece of code is monitoring the child's device mean the child has less right to privacy than if this was an intervention by a human? Surely, this expectation bleeds the responsibilities of the code into the realm of parenting? The relationship between the child and parent could, arguably, be stronger without the parent expecting tools to ensure the child is not misbehaving online.

As a further illustration of the potential ethical abuse and blurred morality that can occur in the drive to achieve more effective image detection systems, we present a more specialist scenario – the detection of child abuse images in law enforcement systems. Within law enforcement there is growing reliance upon machine-learning systems to tackle the proliferation of child abuse images online that is both worthy and concerning[20]. With such volumes there is, of course, a need within law enforcement to have tools to support the role of human analysts in categorising images, initiating takedowns and taking out legal proceedings against hosts and identifying victims, or even the more fundamental issue of whether abuse is taking place and the image can be categorised as illegal. It is well established through technologies such as PhotoDNA[21] that hashing techniques are used effectively in this domain, and can be very useful in detecting existing images and automating the identification process against hash lists. These approaches have been very successful in reducing the need for a human analyst to explore potentially thousands of images down to less than one hundred. However, the fact that they only learn from existing image sets means that they cannot recognise new images that have not been collected and analysed before. Again, we can see that an algorithm being used a as a mechanism within a broader, human-driven, analytical workflow, rather than the complete solution in the problem space, can be extremely successful.

However, there is also a need to recognise and categorise images that have not been classified before, and there is a great deal of interest in the use of machine learning approaches to achieve this. Recent announcements with public/private partnerships between law enforcement and commercial identification platforms[22] have shown that these systems can be a significant aid to the complex and unpleasant task of categorising images of child abuse. Through partnership with law enforcement, the training sets used for the image recognition algorithms can be larger and of greater diversity. In the example given with Griffeye/Taskforce Argos, 300,000 images that had already been categorised by law enforcement professionals were used to train the software, which would, in all probability, improve image-recognition capabilities and reduce the load of human analysts to triage images. However, in the rush to address this undoubtedly honourable intention, perhaps we are, again, raising significant ethical concerns which seem to have had no part in the evolution of these systems.

These algorithms work on images with no care for the content of the image, whereas in reality these are images of children being abused. If the image is a mere unit of analysis is there any consideration of the privacy of the victim in terms of where images are stored, by whom they are accessed, and what meta data exists that might relate to the victim's identity. Given the victims in many images will be identified, do they grant consent for these images to be used in databases, or does ownership on the image reside with the law enforcement partner? While there is clearly a law enforcement need for the image, and it is quite rightly stored in an image database, might we be guilty of placing the need of the law enforcement function ahead of the victim in the image? If the victim has been identified surely they have a right to be aware of where the image is stored and how it is being used?

Perhaps a question that needs to be asked, which seems to have been missing from any debate on the application of technology to this extremely sensitive area, centres around the rights of the victim when examined through machine based, rather than human, intervention? Does the victim have an equal right to privacy if the image is only analysed by an algorithm rather than a human?

There is a growing need for scrutiny in these algorithms, and there seems to be little evidence of this outside of the academic world. We are placing the ethics of safeguarding into the hands of vendors. One of the key issues with these approaches is the lack of independent evaluation of algorithms or their claimed functionality and functional decomposition – in essence there is a lot of money being invested in these areas, and market share to be gained. Therefore there is a great deal of commercial sensitivity among service providers. However, with a lack of transparency and shared IP in this area, arguably progress will be hampered and a lack of accountability will result in the potential for algorithm providers claiming functionality that are perhaps not as effective in reality. And in a field like child safeguarding and protection these can raise potentially serious ethical concerns.

In Chapter 6 we will collect these threads and return to our framework around the rights of the child, asking the question can technology solve all of these issues and still be ethical? Do we see evidence of a more progressive safeguarding environment, or one that continues down a *do more* path without considering the limits of technology or its flaws in addressing social problems.

Notes

1 Hosseinmardi, H., Mattson, S. A., Rafiq, R. I., Han, R., Lv, Q., & Mishra, S. (2015). Detection of cyberbullying incidents on the instagram social network. *arXiv preprint arXiv:1503.03909*.
2 Zhao, R., Zhou, A., & Mao, K. (2016, January). Automatic detection of cyberbullying on social networks based on bullying features. In *Proceedings of the 17th international conference on distributed computing and networking* (p. 43). ACM.
3 Sanchez, H., & Kumar, S. (2011). Twitter bullying detection. *ser. NSDI*, *12*, 15.
4 Card, C. (2018). "How Facebook AI Helps Suicide Prevention". https://newsroom.fb.com/news/2018/09/inside-feed-suicide-prevention-and-ai/
5 BBC News (2014). "Samaritans Pulls 'Suicide Watch' Radar App". www.bbc.co.uk/news/technology-29962199
6 Murphey, M. (2017). "EU Data Laws Block Facebook's Suicide Prevention Tool". www.telegraph.co.uk/technology/2017/11/28/eu-data-laws-block-facebooks-suicide-prevention-tool/
7 O'Neil, C (2016). "Weapons of Math Destruction: How Big Data Increases Inequality and Threatens Democracy." Crown Publishing Group, New York.
8 NSPCC (2018). "Over 3,000 New Grooming Offences Recorded since Last Year". www.nspcc.org.uk/what-we-do/news-opinion/3000-new-grooming-offences/
9 Cano, A. E., Fernandez, M., & Alani, H. (2014, November). Detecting child grooming behaviour patterns on social media. In *International Conference on Social Informatics* (pp. 412–427). Springer, Cham.
10 Bogdanova, D., Rosso, P., & Solorio, T. (2014). "Exploring high-level features for detecting cyberpedophilia". *Computer Speech & Language*, *28*(1), 108–120.
11 Ebrahimi, M., Suen, C. Y., & Ormandjieva, O. (2016). "Detecting predatory conversations in social media by deep convolutional neural networks". *Digital Investigation*, *18*, 33–49.
12 Cox, J. and Koebler, J. (2019). "Why Won't Twitter Treat White Supremacy Like ISIS? Because it Would Mean Banning Some Republican Politicians Too". https://motherboard.vice.com/en_us/article/a3xgq5/why-wont-twitter-treat-white-supremacy-like-isis-because-it-would-mean-banning-some-republican-politicians-too

13 Banks, J. (2010). "Regulating hate speech online". *International Review of Law, Computers & Technology*, 24(3), 233–239.

14 Bursztein, E., Bright, T., Clarke, E., DeLaune, M., Eliff, D.M., Hsu, N., Olson, L., Shehan, J., Thakur, M. & Thomas, K. (2019). "Rethinking the Detection of Child Sexual Abuse Imagery on the Internet". https://storage.googleapis.com/pub-tools-public-publication-data/pdf/04788940adb8e0a244a762a90f19c7a9 4e101b06.pdf

15 Branwen, G. (2019). "The Neural Net Tank Urban Legend". www.gwern.net/Tanks

16 Algorithmia (2016). "Improving Nudity Detection and NSFW Image Recognition". http://blog.algorithmia.com/improving-nudity-detection-nsfw-image-recognition/

17 Peersman, C., Schulze, C., Rashid, A., Brennan, M., & Fischer, C. (2016) "iCOP: Live forensics to reveal previously unknown criminal media on P2P networks". *Digital Investigation*, 18, 50–64.

18 House of Commons Science and Technology Committee (2017). "Impact of social media and screen-use on young people's health". https://publications.parliament.uk/pa/cm201719/cmselect/cmsctech/822/822.pdf

19 UK Government (2008). "Criminal Justice and Immigration Act 2008 Part 5". www.legislation.gov.uk/ukpga/2008/4/part/5

20 Bursztein, E., Bright, T., Clarke, E., DeLaune, M., Eliff, D.M., Hsu, N., Olson, L., Shehan, J., Thakur, M. & Thomas, K. (2019). "Rethinking the Detection of Child Sexual Abuse Imagery on the Internet". https://storage.googleapis.com/pub-tools-public-publication-data/pdf/04788940adb8e0a244a762a90f19c7a9 4e101b06.pdf

21 Microsoft (n.d.). "PhotoDNA". www.microsoft.com/en-us/photodna

22 Griffeye (n.d.). "The New Griffeye AI Technology – Trained at Taskforce Argos". www.griffeye.com/the-griffeye-ai-technology-trained-at-taskforce-argos/

6 Safety at the expense of liberty?

There is a quote from a letter by Benjamin Franklin, one of the founding fathers of the United States of America, often used by digital libertarians to argue that rights should not be trumped by safety[1]:

> Those who would give up essential Liberty, to purchase a little temporary Safety, deserve neither Liberty nor Safety.

While the origins of the quote certainly have little to do with the relinquishing of liberty in order to keep us, or our children, safe, it is a useful set of words to make use of and reflect upon whether, in our rush to ensure our population is safe from the harms of the internet, and our reliance on code to achieve this, we might be removing fundamental rights and moving toward the *safeguarding dystopia*. Clearly, there is a balance between safety and liberty, particularly when that safety cannot be clearly articulated and defined in law. However, we might observe that some technologies that argue a safeguarding rationale, fall short of this goal and are, arguably, more about control and surveillance.

In this book we have critically examined the technologies used in the online safeguarding of children and young people and explored the extent to which technology can be applied to boundaryless social problems. We have done this analysis against a policy backdrop that has expected platform providers and vendors to present solutions to the issues that arise from the social use of technology, and showed how this policy has moved from a specific type of content management to wide-ranging calls to prevent children from being exposed to all manner of online harms. In this final chapter, we review the technologies available in the safeguarding portfolio and consider whether the balance between intrusion and rights is fair and effective, and whether this technologically fixated policy direction is actually addressing the problems it claims to be trying to address.

This closing chapter reflects on what potentially could become a dystopian dogma of safeguarding, where the use of algorithms with a justification of keeping children risk-free ultimately results in children who have no privacy, constant surveillance, reduced access to information and media, and utterly fails to achieve Article 3 of the UN Convention of the Rights of the Child. Paragraph 3 of this article states:

Parties shall ensure that the institutions, services and facilities responsible for the care or protection of children shall conform with the standards established by competent authorities, particularly in the areas of safety, health, in the number and suitability of their staff, as well as competent supervision.

Handing over the online welfare of children to private sector organisations, with little scrutiny, to offer solutions to safeguarding that hang more on the collection of any data the child generates through their online lives, and policy pressure, and do so in order to make a profit, does not seem like the best interests of the child are paramount. While we do not suggest in the slightest that the might be some vendors in the child safeguarding space who place profit ahead of ethical practice, there is potential, in an unregulated domain where scrutiny of algorithms is non-existent, and with an almost complete opacity of the algorithms function (and even how they were developed and tested), can we really be confident that the best interest of the child are at the heart of any decision made and the functionality proposed has been thorough and exhaustively tested?

Returning to the stakeholder model in Chapter 1 (see Figure 1.1), the focus of the vast majority of policy detail in recent times has been the Exosystem, almost entirely ignoring the microsystems around the child, except to call for those actors in the Exosystem to *do more* to support those in the microsystem.

By way of illustration of this point, it is worthwhile to review a recent world-wide online safety incident where stakeholders within the microsystems all engaged, perhaps to the detriment of the young people they purported to keep safe. While a more detailed examination of the Momo "suicide game" has been written elsewhere[2], the salient points are explored below in relation to the role of stakeholders in the microsystems and also how algorithms were powerless to intervene when those stakeholders within the microsystem failed in their safe-guarding approach.

From February 25 to March 2 2019, the UK saw what we might regard as a moral panic hitting both social media and traditional news outlets related to a digital phenomenon called *Momo*. This was reportedly another online suicide game[3] that was encouraging children to self-harm and kill themselves. According to the zeitgeist, the *Momo challenge* placed a disturbing image (actually a photograph of a sculpture of an *ubume* produced by the artist Keisuke Aisawa[4] in 2016) that appeared in videos, that would be watched by young children (such as popular cartoon characters like Peppa Pig). Alongside the image was an audio track, that would instruct the viewer to contact a mobile phone number, which would then set up a series of challenges for the victim, which involved instructions to self-harm and demands to commit suicide. Quite why the young children who would generally be watching these videos would even possess a mobile phone, let alone respond to instructions to contact a number, was not explored in the reporting of this new digital outrage. However, what was reported was that the challenge had been linked to the suicides of children in Argentina, Mexico, and India[5]. Obviously a very worrying premise for anyone with children who were more inclined to a knee jerk reaction than a proper investigation of the accuracy of the reporting and social media posts.

YouTube was, predictably, called upon to prevent Momo images from appearing. After all, it was proclaimed, their platform was one of the ones used to disseminate this dangerous game, and therefore they should stop it. We should stress that this was not an organised attempt to cause harm. This was something used by online trolls to scare children by injecting an upsetting image, potentially alongside some audio instructions, into a random and child-centric video. Algorithmically, this presents a challenge – even if the same Momo image was used in all videos, it would considerable processing to run through all content to detect a single frame. Not impossible, but very difficult, processor intensive, and arguably not a good use of a platform's resources, particularly a platform that, we should bear in mind, already provides reporting routes for anyone who sees anything upsetting.

YouTube's response was very factual and measured[6]:

> Many of you have shared your concerns with us over the past few days about the Momo Challenge – we've been paying close attention to these reports. After much review, we've seen no recent evidence of videos promoting the Momo Challenge on YouTube.

Momo had been of interest to those of us who explore these *digital ghost stories* since 2018, and most ignored it for what it is – a hoax taken up by various online trolls who wish to scare children by placing the image in child-centric videos alongside a few poorly crafted messages, done to generate views, hits on their content, and possibly gain some notoriety by upsetting children along the way.

Therefore, it was something of a surprise to see it so significantly hit the headlines in late February 2019. Public outrage followed, with calls by celebrities, online safety companies, academics, police, schools, and the news media for social media providers (particularly YouTube) to do the responsible thing and control the spread of the (fictitious) challenge on their platforms.

We can see almost identical public hysteria around another digital ghost story that had occurred a couple of years earlier. The Blue Whale Challenge[7] had a near identical modus operandi (although with this one the alleged suicides were occurring in Russian) which, on investigation, proved to have been entirely unfounded.

Then, the Doki Doki Literature Club, an interactive video game with psychological horror story threads, was cited by a coroner in the North West[8] of England as being linked to the tragic suicide of Ben Walmsley. As a result of this warning many police forces issued alerts that were then sent to schools and, via social media, to parents. Parents then shared these concerns on social media, and many children were asked about a game they had never played, and subsequently search for, based on one comment by a coroner. If we were to take an objective perspective, we would have seen that the game had been downloaded over

2 million times[9]. A single mention of implied causation, against those statistics, does not hold out to scrutiny.

In all three of these cases the spread of "awareness" was virtually identical – media reporting, comment from "responsible" bodies, social media spread, public outcry, then more rational comment in order to calm the hysteria.

From a safeguarding perspective, while the Momo challenge is entirely fake as an organised operation aiming to get children to self-harm or commit suicide, it is also evident that online trolls and meme creators are willing to inject in the image and upsetting dialogue into children's videos for young people to stumble across. As such, children can still see the, clearly disturbing, image and will become upset when they see and hear instructions telling them to hurt themselves or that others might get harmed. If we raise awareness of these stories, whether real or fake, it will result in vulnerable children getting upset and concerned by what they have seen. There is a clear need for both news outlets and responsible bodies to act in a manner that explores the credibility of the sources to these stories, and the wider evidence base. We now have a history of how these digital ghost stories emerge, yet still these bodies respond in a reactive, hysterical way.

In the week of the Momo hype wave, we achieved a near perfect storm of news coverage, celebrity social media commentary, and online safety organisations all wishing to become the main player in solving this non-existent crisis. Perhaps the biggest trigger for the spike in interest came when the Police Service of Northern Ireland produced a press release in 2019 that raised serious concerns about the potential harm the Momo challenge posed[10]. Highlights of this press release included:

> 'Whilst no official reports have been made to Police, we are aware of the so-called "Momo" challenge and are already liaising with other UK Police Services to try to identify the extent of the problem and to look for opportunities to deal with this issue'.

> 'This extremely disturbing challenge conceals itself within other harmless looking games or videos played by children and when downloaded, it asks the user to communicate with "Momo" via popular messaging applications such as WhatsApp. It is at this point that children are threatened that they will be cursed or their family will be hurt if they do not self-harm'.

> 'I am disgusted that a so-called game is targeting our young children and I would encourage parents to know what your children are looking at and who they are talking to'.

This release, coming from a source of authority, legitimised the reporting from the more tabloid end of news outlets, and other stakeholders in child safeguarding and then triggered a social media storm using these authoritative sources which parents, concerned about their children's safety, then propagated further. Awareness raising resources were provided by some online safety organisations talking about how to tackle the Momo challenge (which, we need to bear in mind, doesn't exist), and these resources were shared by concerned individuals on social media, therefore driving the Momo challenge further into the public consciousness. All of this resulted in many children being made aware of Momo, and of course they then went off to search for it online.

Data collected from NGO partners showed a 45,000% increase in searches for Momo in schools during "Momo week". The awareness raising carried out by stakeholders in children's safeguarding resulted in, unsurprisingly, young people becoming concerned about Momo and therefore searching for it and conversely discovering upsetting images. In the survey described in Chapter 2, as already discussed, we asked young people whether they have seen anything online that has upset them. Unsurprisingly, since Momo week, there have been 22 disclosures relating to it (with 21 of those responses coming from primary aged children), from 495 responses in all. Prior to Momo week there were no mentions of Momo among the 9,106 responses we had received.

In this incident, we can see that in conflict with what we should expect from adult stakeholders around online safety, where they should be ensuring children are not exposed to harmful content or, if this impossible dream cannot be achieved at least mitigating risks and supporting harm reduction, young people were actively driven toward the harmful content, through poorly thought out education strategy and hysterical response. While there remained calls for YouTube to "do more", the reality was that many young people were exposed to this upsetting image because adults, in their rush to publicise this suicide game, failed to adopt fundamental and well-considered approaches to supporting children and young people online. There is certainly nothing illegal about the Momo image and while perhaps discomforting, there is nothing either sexually or violently explicit. The simple message to children and young people remains "If you see something that upsets you online, tell us about it", not "theres this thing called Momo and under no circumstances should you look for it". Returning to our stakeholder model in Chapter 1, those with greatest impact on young people's safeguarding are the ones most responsible for promoting awareness of Momo to young people. And we can clearly see, in our evidence, that it had a very clear impact.

In their Online Harms white paper, the UK government defined "the challenge" of online harms to be:

- Illegal and unacceptable content and activity is widespread online, and UK users are frequently concerned about what they have seen or experienced.
- The prevalence of the most serious illegal content and activity on the internet, which threatens our national security or the physical safety of children, is unacceptable. The ease and extremity of the most serious online offending such as child sexual exploitation and abuse (CSEA) continues to increase.
- The impact of harmful content and activity can be particularly damaging for children and young people, and there are growing concerns about the potential impact on their mental health and wellbeing.
- Tackling illegal and harmful content and activity online is one part of the UK's wider mission to develop rules and norms for the internet, including protecting personal data, supporting competition in digital markets and promoting responsible digital design.

And sets out proposals for a regulatory framework around which companies who provide online services have a *duty of care* toward their users to ensure they are free from harm and that companies *that allow users to share or discover user-generated content or interact with each other online* will fall under this framework. It expects companies to "invest in the development of safety technologies to reduce the burden on users to stay safe online".

Yet if we are to reflect on the Momo incident and the impact that had on young people, we question what either duty of care by platform providers or a regulator would have been able to do about these videos being posted. One thing they might do is call for the sort of measures that would kill any aspect of user-generated content online and be an impossible resource implication for companies (i.e. full human moderation prior to posting). YouTube reports[11] 300 hours of video uploaded per minute, along with over 5 billion videos shared to date. Human moderation of all of this content prior to posting is an almost impossible task, and is certainly an impossible expectation. YouTube have, along with most other platform providers, adopted a community model instead, by providing the means for users of the platform to report harmful content, which can then be moderated and removed if deemed harmful. This works similarly to physical spaces with significant throughput, such as railway stations, where it would be impossible to search everyone entering the space, but there are plenty of warning and alerts to those using the spaces to report anything suspicious and it can then be dealt with. There is a collective responsibility for safety, rather than expecting the security and safety for the space to be entirely the responsibility of those working at the station. That is not to say there isn't more the providers could do – we speak to many young people who do not believe reporting works, because those who have attempted it rarely see any rectification of issues arising from the reports. Companies could, clearly *do more* in terms of speed of response and transparency of reporting, and we welcome the calls in the Online Harms white paper to require providers to provide yearly transparency report.

However, the general policy direction is still an expectation to provide increasing numbers of technical tools, eroding more and more rights and freedoms, in order to keep children and young people safe.

We have, within this text, explored a range of "safeguarding" technologies, such as:

- Content filtering – preventing access to "harmful" content by filtering based upon keyword matching
- Site blocking – preventing access to "harmful" content by filtering based upon URL matching
- Access monitoring – determining authority to access a given site, which may contain harmful content, via some form of authentication (for example, age verification)
- Behavioural monitoring – using keyword matching techniques and natural language processing to determine how an individual is behaviour on a platform for device

- Interaction monitoring – explicitly collecting data on interactions passed to authority figures (for example parents or teachers)
- Location tracking – determining the location of an individual via GPS tracking technology via mobile device
- Image matching – matching an image to another and determining similarity based upon hashing technologies
- Image recognition – determining the nature of an image using machine learning technology

The vast majority of these technologies, if used excessively and without critical thought, can negatively impact on children's rights.

We have seen where technology works, and why, and also when it fails, and why. Yet it is difficult to see whether even the most tightly packed functional arsenal of home safeguarding technologies would solve an issue like Momo. Because fundamentally, the failing there lay with those responsible for the child's safeguarding, not the delivery platform.

While algorithms *can* have an extremely positive role to play in child protection and safeguarding, they can also have a significant impact upon the rights of the child and potentially other actors within social systems. We have to balance the value of algorithms, and the strengths of code, with the need for greater professional knowledge, education, and policy understanding if these techniques are going to be used effectively and proportionately, with a child-centric perspective that looks to protect them from risk and harm while being cognisant of their rights. And we will only achieve this is those making and shaping policy understand where the strengths of code lie, and what it is less capable of achieving.

On the 25th anniversary of the World Wide Web in 2014, Tim Berners Lee, its founder, was interviewed about what he thought were the important policy issues facing digital technology in the future[12]. In a wide-ranging interview, among other things, he stated:

'Our rights are being infringed more and more on every side, and the danger is that we get used to it. So I want to use the 25th anniversary for us all to do that, to take the web back into our own hands and define the web we want for the next 25 years … . But we need our lawyers and our politicians to understand programming, to understand what can be done with a computer'.

Within the online safeguarding policy area, there seems to be scant appreciation around how code, or the *Lex Informatica*, works. There is little understanding that software code, and its formation into algorithms, can only apply rules to a situation and determine outcomes based on those rules. When terms such as artificial intelligence are used ad nauseum by policy makers, they have little grasp of *how* code is constructed and believe that these are big developments in the technological field, a domain that makes the impossible possible. Rather than appreciating this as a field with a rich history of application, it is seen as being made up of narrow domains with clearly defined rule sets, and without the deployment of socially ambiguous, unconstrained, and unpredictable spaces. Software systems work within boundaries, not open spaces. One cannot simply wave one's hand and claim something is possible is code. If something is difficult to define in a logical process flow or to model in mathematics, it is unlikely that a technological solution is possible.

In our rush to automate these processes, we are failing to acknowledge the role of the human in these scenarios – understanding nuances around social behaviour, cultural differences and, perhaps most importantly, context. An algorithm will be extremely well at determining whether a word is in a sentence. It is less good at determining the tone of the sentence, the intention of the writer's message, or the history of communication in which that message sits. Morality in an algorithm can only exist in the transference of morality from the developer to the code, and its coding in logic. While the morality of the developer might be driven by personal beliefs, equally it might come from the policy of the company. And that policy might, of itself, be driven from the interests of the organisation. Which will in turn be driven by market forces, political pressures, and legislation. The ability to exercise discretion is lost in this interpretation, and instead we end up dealing with literals in code in a field where subtlety, empathy, and pragmatism are important.

If, as we claim in this text, algorithms will only ever be part of a solution, or a tool for safeguarding, we are lead to the question – "What would work then?".

We have many conversations with young people about what adults could do to best help them navigate the online worlds in which they are growing up. They invariably respond with three requirements:

Listen, don't judge, and understand.

An algorithm is neither capable of listening or understanding. And while it is certainly capable of not judging, equally it will form its morality around those who have encoded it, with their unconscious biases and interpretations of requirements of the algorithms. The nature of the *safeguarding dystopia* is one where a child will not engage in risk-taking behaviours because they know they are being watched, tracked, or monitored, where prohibition is viewed as safer than addressing the impacts of online harm.

If we are to take, by way of example, the policy direction around pornography, it has always been focussed upon how we stop children from viewing this content, rather than addressing the fact they do. We, as adults with safeguarding responsibilities, do not want the difficult conversation so we try to prevent them happening. We feed an adultist agenda that believes we *have* to control the online lives of children and young people based upon poorly understood perspectives on how they use online technologies. The Digital Harms White Paper assumes a passive child who has harmful content thrown at them in various forms, with them unable to deal with these harms themselves. Yet young people tell us they are active participants in the online world, for many different reasons. Most of them positive and harmless.

However, because there are awkward issues that might arise, such as young people accessing pornography, sometime voluntarily, sometimes voraciously, we would rather hope that someone can prevent this from happening, rather than acknowledging it does and implementing education strategies that allow young people to develop critical thinking around the subject matter. While sites like Pornhub celebrate more than ten years in the online world, there are still a dearth of education resources for pornography. We would rather hope the technology sector can come up with solutions, using the only raw materials available to them – data and code. And because there are limits to what that is capable of, they fall short of ever changing and increasingly complex requirements, and code becomes the scapegoat in the safeguarding scenario. While Lessig stated that in cyberspace, code is law, what he was stating that the only way to regulate digital communication, and its underpinning algorithms, was using code. Other regulation would fail. However, this isn't to say that the behaviours that are facilitated by online can *only* be regulated with code. Just as legislation to tackle hate speech is as applicable online than offline, there are ways to tackle safeguarding offline that are equally valid online – such as well trained, and informed stakeholders around the child, effective education, understanding of risk for young people, and open, clear, and transparent reporting routes that are responsive. However, policy still, it seems, would rather demand code is used to solve all of the problems and applied in circumstances with which it struggles. We control, rather than support, and place the child at the centre of the digital panopticon, hoping this will make them safe.

Part 1(d) of Article 29 on the UN Convention of the Rights of the Child (the Goals of Education) starts by stating that "states parties agree that the education of the child shall be directed to":

The preparation of the child for responsible life in a free society.

If through our wish to ensure they are safe (and docile), we become increasingly controlling, through algorithms that are seen as the solution to online safeguarding but can only process information and make judgement based upon interpretation of this information and, as a result, restrict a child's access to information, media, online relationships and online expression, are we really fulfilling this commitment?

Notes

1 Founders Online (n.d.). "Pennsylvania Assembly: Reply to the Governor". https://founders.archives.gov/documents/Franklin/01-06-02-0107
2 Phippen, A. and Bond, E. (2019). "Digital Ghost Stories; Impact, Risks and Reasons". https://swgfl.org.uk/assets/documents/digital-ghost-stories-impact-risks-and-reasons-1.pdf
3 Mukhra, R., Baryah, N., Krishan, K., & Kanchan, T. (2019). "Blue Whale Challenge': A game or crime?". *Science and Engineering Ethics*, 25(1), 285–291.
4 Instagram (2016). "Between Mirrors – Mother Bird". www.instagram.com/p/BlQlfA2Biju/

5 *The Sun* (2019). "SUICIDE WARNING: What is the Momo Challenge, Is there a UK Number and How Many Deaths Has It Been Linked to?" www.thesun. co.uk/news/6926762/what-momo-suicide-game-whatsapp-deaths-uk-hoax/

6 Google (2019). "Our Response to the Momo Challenge & Character". https:// support.google.com/youtube/thread/1917881?hl=en

7 Wikipedia (n.d.). "Blue Whale Challenge". https://en.wikipedia.org/wiki/ Blue_Whale_Challenge

8 *The Sun* (2018). "SUICIDE WARNING What is the Doki Doki Literature Club and Why Have Schools Issued a Warning to Parents over the DDLC Online Game?"/ www.thesun.co.uk/news/6630711/doki-doki-literature-club-police-school-warning-suicide/

9 Jomes, A. (2018). "Doki Doki Literature Club! Surpasses Two Million Download". www.pcgamesn.com/doki-doki-literature-club/doki-doki-litera-ture-club-player-numbers

10 PSNI (2019). "PSNI Statement regarding Momo Challenge" www.psni.police. uk/news/Latest-News/250219-psni-statement-regarding-momo-challenge/

11 Omnicore Agency (2019). "YouTube by the Numbers: Stats, Demographics & Fun Facts". www.omnicoreagency.com/youtube-statistics/

12 Kiss, J. (2014). "An Online Magna Carta: Berners-Lee Calls for Bill of Rights for Web". www.theguardian.com/technology/2014/mar/12/online-magna-carta-berners-lee-web

Index

For Product Safety Concerns and Information please contact our EU
representative GPSR@taylorandfrancis.com
Taylor & Francis Verlag GmbH, Kaufingerstraße 24, 80331 München, Germany

www.ingramcontent.com/pod-product-compliance
Ingram Content Group UK Ltd.
Pitfield, Milton Keynes, MK11 3LW, UK
UKHW021437080625
459435UK00011B/287